It was a snowy Sunday morning when my friend came knocking on my door. She wasn't bundled in a heavy winter coat with hat and scarf and woolly mittens on her hands; all she had on were pyjamas, a jacket and untied snow boots. Her hair was wind blown and snow covered. In her hand she held a **tea rose**.

It was the strangest juxtaposition! There I stood in the doorway, transfixed and unable to move. But it was not the cold weather conditions that kept me frozen in my tracks...it was her smile. Soon I felt none of the cold and all of the calm and comfort it radiated.

"Well, aren't you going to invite me in?" she asked mischievously, while stepping past me into the room. Before peeling off her jacket and removing her boots, she handed me the tea rose.

I stood there mesmerised by the freshness of the bloom; I could feel moisture on the top of my hand from a dew drop... "It's incredible, isn't it?" queried Elsie. "Incredible!" I uttered.

"When I woke up this morning," she began, "it was from an unpleasant and frightening dream. I couldn't even remember what it was about, but I'm sure of the residue of emotion left behind. I felt an uncontrollable urge to weep, and so I did....Finally, the weeping ended and I got up and walked to my bedroom window. While I stood there watching and listening to the blowing snow... something caught my eye.

Unable to make out what it was, I quickly climbed into my snow boots, grabbed a jacket, and went outside to investigate. It was difficult to navigate through the whirling snow and the dim light of dawn. **Then I saw it. So alone it stood...the bloom as fresh as a new spring morning.**

The leaves provided a delightful contrast to the whiteness of the ground cover; but nothing could have prepared me for the truly surprising **tea rose...a magnificent bloom of colour and vibrancy**. I bent down to take a closer look and what I saw reflected in those iridescent petals made my heart wild with love! Looking back at me was you, Sandra, pouring a cup of tea, a cup of love and friendship."

This is my story and I'm sipping it!

Published by Writing For The Love Of It Publishing, September 2022
ISBN: 9781778272905

Copyright © 2021 by Sandra Davis
All rights reserved. No part of this publication may be reproduced, stored in or introduced into a retrieval system, or transmitted, in any form, or by any means (electronic, mechanical, photocopying, recording or otherwise) without the prior written permission of the publisher. This book is sold subject to the condition that it shall not, by way of trade or otherwise, be lent, resold, hired out, or otherwise circulated without the publisher's prior consent in any form of binding or cover other than that in which it is published and without a similar condition including this condition being imposed on the subsequent purchaser.

Editor: Emma Pickering
Typeset: Greg Salisbury
Book Cover Design: Emma Pickering
Photographer: Elsie Poliquin

DISCLAIMER: Readers of this publication agree that neither Sandra Davis, Elsie Poliquin, nor the publisher will be held responsible or liable for damages that may be alleged as resulting directly or indirectly from the use of this publication. Neither the publisher nor the author can be held accountable for the information provided by, or actions, resulting from, accessing these resources.

Once upon a time there was a meeting place. A refuge of sorts from anything ordinary. Hospitality graced every aspect of this exceptional dwelling. From its homespun kitchen with heady aromas of simmering Borscht to fresh baked bread, garden salad and mouth-watering desserts. The old kitchen table was dressed for company, in a cheerful patterned cloth of yellow daisies. A jarful of fresh cut flowers, handmade plates, mugs, and serving dishes moulded and shaped by an artisan's hand, graced this bygone table of plenty.

Spring, Summer, Autumn and Winter…each ancient Season acknowledged and celebrated in this remarkable place. Spring-times that burst tenaciously from sleepy bulbs, dormant through short but steady winter months of mainland B.C. Crocus, wild trilliums, and tulips, erupting from earth with will and determination; reminiscent of a birthing calf…yes! Flowers calving, breaking up and out. Much like the women who gravitate here. Renewing, recharging, and expanding with the ancients…

Summer with early morning breezes warmed by a giant mango-sun, rising unimpeded in the sky. A pileated woodpecker hammering on a distant tree; rat-a-tat-tat, rat-a-tat-tat multitasking for breakfast and for territory! Breath-taking profusions of lilac purples, hot pink hydrangea, yellow daisies with darkened faces, and white flowering apple blossoms…sights and smells that intoxicate.

Autumn, not trailing but blazing in on a painter's brush! Precision strokes abandoned; spillage and splashes of crimson red, tangerine orange, and glorious yellows erupting in a plethora of colour…bursting…then dying and fizzling out.

On those blustery Winter days when the ocean was most formidable, our greeting was the warmth and crackling melody of a wood burning fire. Even the furniture beckoned… imperially draped in homespun blankets and cheery fleece throws.

Here is where it really began.

Our little group of women gathered to dine and laugh and share experiences while lounging on the sofa or in one of the overstuffed rockers, sipping herbal tea or Sherry; the most we could attempt after such flagrant indulgence! Basking in the warmth and comfort of this room, this place and each other. A by-product of which was the creation of this book…a true collaboration by the feminine.

Angels *really* do the darndest things!

Inga's 80th birthday, from left to right: Linda, Sandra, Inga, Elsie, & Aliyana.

How is it that we entertained the notion of a book about Angel Dolls? I would suspect it was a night like this one. An evening with Elsie. An evening of friends…talking, laughing, and reflecting on this amazing journey.

'Twas a night like this that Elsie read us a letter; one that had just arrived in the mail. It was an enchanting story shared by one of Elsie's newest clients, with regards to her most personal experience of the Angel

Doll sculpture she had commissioned. The story was warm and wonderful, happy, and emotional, laced with just the right amount of humour.

A spark of excitement was lit in each of us! Discussions ensued with unbridled enthusiasm for Angel Doll stories received and shared, which included first-hand experiences of our own.

Well! It soon appeared evident to me, to all of us, that sharing these Angel Doll stories was definitive. Our personal experience of this evening was one of healing…just by listening to these anecdotes. This became the catalyst for gathering other stories and for their future dissemination.

As a group, we were determined to spend more evenings communicating our desire for a book about angels. Elsie was thrilled with the idea of sharing these distinctive narratives but was clear that she was not prepared to draft a book. So, it was I that accepted the baton.

I mean really! It only felt right to expose the rareness of personalised Angel Dolls and the impact they had on the people who receive them. It is with this sense of responsibility and my immense respect for the creator and custodian of our meeting place; Custodian, as 14229 Marine Drive was Elsie's rental home while living in White Rock, BC. And Creator; as in her being the decorator, designer, and gardener in this ocean view paradise.

Elsie was imprinted on this address. The natural life-giving force that made for this magical place completely aligned with Elsie's *energy*[i] and that of the angels. Every inch of this home was living and breathing creativity, a true example of Elsie manifested in the world. So, too, were the Angel Dolls she sculpted into being. Together they inspired me to honour their contribution by creating a book where a collection of personal Angel Doll experiences could be compiled and shared as stories, along with pictures of many of her unique sculptures.

One such experience happens while I'm driving along Vancouver's King Edward Boulevard. I'm dazzled! Or maybe just dazed? The sun, warming the ocean breeze wafting through my open window is courted by music from the radio "Riding along in my automobile…"

And just as I'm about to reach the traffic lights at 'Arbutus'…I see it! I can't quite believe it, but I really do see it.

Angels really *do the darndest things!*

A giant billboard! Right there in the middle of the old railway plot. When did they put that up? And what's with the Monk? It reads: St. Francis Xavier. Who? The only Xavier I know of is Xavier Cugat.[1] Oh, darn! The lights turned green, and I've got to turn!

I continue my drive to my friend's house knowing I'm just minutes away from Maple Street; after all this is my intended destination. Fortunately for me, my friend is an excellent teacher and has lived in Vancouver most of her adult life. If anyone knows when and why the billboard was put up, she will.

The first words out of my mouth when I walked through her door were, "Hi there, do you know who St. Francis Xavier is?"

"Who?" she asked.

"Some guy who I think is a monk," I replied, "and is named St. Francis Xavier?"

"The name does sound familiar," she responded. "But I can't be certain. Perhaps the computer at the library would be helpful?"

"No, if he's not familiar to you, I'll call my sister back east. She seems to be doing a lot of research these days; perhaps she can find some information about this guy."

"Why this particular monk and why now?" asked my friend.

"Well, I'm just curious. I mean till today I never noticed that giant billboard at King Edward and Arbutus. And since the only thing on the sign was the picture of a monk with the name St. Francis Xavier…I thought you of all people would know what it's about. Didn't you tell me that you went to a Catholic girl's school?"

"Hold on a minute! You're telling me there's a billboard on the old railway property at the corner of Arbutus?"

To summarise, let me just say that my friend was even more surprised than me and at a total loss regarding this new development of a billboard in her neighbourhood!

---

[1] *Spanish Musician 1900-1990*

Angel Doll St. Francis Xavier in Elsie's Garden

The following day this same friend was planning to collect my left-handed golf clubs. She had secured a buyer for them and was to deliver the clubs in person. When she arrived at my place that morning…she was not very happy! It turns out that my friend went out of her way to drive by the new billboard at King Edward and Arbutus.

Angels really *do the darndest things!*

Imagine if you will, her *bewilderment* at finding no such sign! The old, abandoned railway plot was exactly as it had been for years. Nothing on it. Zero. Zilch. Nada.

"Ridiculous, that's absolutely ridiculous!" was my indignant reaction. "You drive, I'm coming with you, we'll drive over together…It has to be there…I couldn't possibly imagine a giant billboard!!!"

No billboard. No sign. The old, abandoned railway plot is as overgrown and unattended as ever. It has finally happened; I've gone round the bend. I'm beginning to see things that are not there. I shake my head in absolute dismay all the way back home. My friend has now calmed down and is doing her best to console me.

The next day I regrouped and called my sister back east, to investigate the matter further. Her research provided some rather interesting information. Apparently, story goes that Francis Xavier and Ignatius Loyola had been noblemen who felt that everyone should have access to education:

> "Francis Xavier, ST. (b.1506-d.1552) …... Francis became one of the seven who in 1534, at Montmartre founded the society of Jesus ORDER OF THE JESUITS!"[ii]

What I truly gleaned through Xavier's decision to introduce himself by way of the billboard, is his capacity for humour, and I was reminded of this quote:

"Choosing to laugh when tangled in your own seriousness can immediately diffuse the stranglehold of anger and judgments, self-importance, and inflexibility. Once your rigidity is removed, you are free to again integrate the present set of circumstances, finding what you may have formerly overlooked."[2]

This situation taught me how to trust and laugh at myself…a rare kindness indeed.

---

[2] Medicine Cards-Alligator Medicine- by Jamie Sams & David Carson, St. Martin's Press, New York page 237

The Giver of Gifts

The Giver of Gifts is a reference that the Angels chose for Elsie, and one that became apparent to all who met her or were blessed to receive her fascinating creations. The Angels' participation in motivating and guiding Elsie's hands, her heart, and her *divine* intelligence are evident in the physical manifestation of her Angel Dolls; like that of Michael Angelo's 'David' they appear divinely inspired.

Elsie acknowledged the angels' insight into the nature of humanity and allowed it to be the catalyst for creating these angel sculptures. Their physical appearance being life-like, instead of porcelain perfection, provided a true sense of the familiar. Humanity comes in many shapes and sizes. Skin, hair, eyes, body shape and size differ demographically and historically.

At the onset of this unique project, it became clear to Elsie that her intention must be aligned with that of the angels. Her contribution in the form of physical manifestations of our angels so that we may relate on a more personal level seemed a true alliance. Elsie came to an understanding that humanity is best served with a hands-on approach to *divinity*. The *divine* aspect of angels lives within all of us. Coming to know one's *Angel-Self*, can best be achieved by establishing a relationship of intimacy and respect with the angels.

An Angel Doll SCULPTURE

I am now interpreting Elsie's own narrative. She describes her experience in creating the original Angel Doll as follows:

During my participation in a workshop, one that I was invited to join, I had an epiphany! It was a voice inside my head: *You, Elsie Mary, will make Angel Dolls. You will sculpt them and adorn them with magnificent wings and thought-provoking costumes. Through this process each Angel Doll you create will be aligning with their intended. This alignment awakens a remembering of the angelic realm in their personal lives. The guidance each of these Angel Dolls provides will be as unique and individual as the recipients.*

For my initial experience of sculpting and designing an Angel Doll creation, I felt guided and directed. This was my first real exposure to the existence of a *'knowing'*. This *knowing* was clear! The *Angel vibration* I was working with was that of an older and wiser male *energy*. As I continued to sculpt my creation I chose to trust and allow the individual direction from the angels. This was to become my methodology for all future creations.

The Angel Doll I was sculpting was a gift for my teacher, the facilitator of the workshop. As the completion of my sculpture drew near, my youngest daughter chose to give some unsolicited advice!

"Mom, this Angel is chubbier than you've made him."

"No," I said, "angels aren't fat."

She then proceeded to tell me, "He doesn't have that much hair."

"No," I said, "angels aren't bald!"

So it was that I continued to work on this Angel Doll, silently claiming, *this is my creation, clear out, no trespassing allowed!*

Now on reflection I can look back and admire my daughter's insight and the benefit of receiving it. A child is unencumbered by the dense energy that I, as an adult, carried. The significance of this process in removing the veils of *density* from my perception enabled me to expand exponentially!

The day arrived to present my completed Angel Doll to my teacher Linda. There was a workshop with her that weekend, and I was running behind schedule. The reason for my tardiness was due in fact to OPHILIUS, the Angel Doll I was gifting to my teacher. He was insisting on some last-minute changes!

Meanwhile, my teacher shared with the group that although I would be late, the angels had asked her not to begin until I arrived. And so it was that I presented the gift of my creation to my teacher.

Her initial response, "Oh, that's so nice Elsie, thank you" soon became a gasp.

"Oh my gosh that's the Angel OPHILIUS! However, OPHILIUS is a bit heavier and doesn't have that much hair." I had created the Angel Doll OPHILIUS in his unique *vibration* WOW!

When my teacher let out a gasp, so too did another participant by the name of Sandra, totally convinced that she too knew this angel…she claimed the angel had just shown himself to her in the weeks before the workshop, and in the strangest possible way. In Sandra's words:

"I was sitting in the living room of a friend having a conversation, when suddenly I found myself (*energetically*) sitting in the back of a stretch limousine. In the front seat the driver was all dressed up in his limousine livery, with white wiry hair sticking out beneath his cap. Slowly turning round his eyes met mine…blue and sparkling like the Ionian Sea, alive and dancing with unbridled merriment! A smile that graduated, from mischievous to infectious, while holding me captive. I couldn't help myself, I started laughing uncontrollably. In fact, I was still laughing when I realized my friend was yelling at me! 'Why on earth are you laughing?' Needless to say, I told her verbatim what had just occurred."

Angel Doll OPHILIUS

Sandra's story and my teacher, Linda's, firsthand exposure to the Angel OPHILIUS affirmed how I felt about my Angel Doll… and the insightful contribution of my youngest daughter Ella Dawn. The Angel OPHILIUS had made his personal introductions. And though I personally had no previous knowledge of OPHILIUS, he soon became an integral part of my support, and that of many others.

An Angel Doll sculpture

My next Angel Doll developed as the result of a commission I received. So began the process again…trusting in my *knowing*, asking questions when I needed clarification, and listening for guidance. I don't seem to recall ever asking the question of myself, "How do you think you can do this?" I just did it.

Through the process of making these Angel Dolls in a person's unique *vibration*, there are details that I am guided to incorporate; a particular costume and its style, the importance of colour, the appropriate adornments…all these details somehow propel the recipient to open up to a personal remembering of the *divine*.

Sometimes the *energy* becomes difficult for me to work in, due to its *density*. When this happens, I cease the work I am currently on and wait. I innately know that the necessary components have not *aligned*, and my timing must be allowed to *synchronize* with that of the *universe*. I continue to wait until motivated by an understanding of *divine inspiration*.

The Giver of Gifts

Angel Doll URANUIS

As I look back at this amazing journey, I can see this was not an easy time in my life. Here I was middle aged, divorced, and raising a daughter on my own. No stable job or career to fall back on, and all the usual fears, besetting a woman in my position. Furthermore, I could no longer accept my old life as any kind of blueprint for the future. I had no formal artistic-training and limited sculpting experience, but others in my life certainly supported me. I live in gratitude and thank God for the assistance I received from all *realms* during this time.

I recall a time many years ago when I was sitting at my desk creating an Angel sculpture for someone in Toronto. In my mind I can see this amazing light pouring through the window in my workshop while a statement resounds in my head: "Through the creation of these Angel Dolls I am releasing *personal mind-sets* of God." Imagine that!

In the process of designing and sculpting these Angel Dolls, the wings and costumes became an issue for me. The wings proved to be especially time consuming. So began an investigation into 'artistic venues' throughout Canada and the United States, in search of an alternative.

It became my opinion that there must be professionals who were better suited to do this part of my creation than I was. All the time I was searching, I consistently asked the question, "Will I find acceptable wings?" The answer I received was a resounding, "Yes!"

Well, after many miles, and hours of research, the light bulb of creativity came on! The 'acceptable wings' that I had been assured I would find, were, to use the proverbial phrase from Dorothy in The Wizard of Oz[3], "Right in my own backyard." The sculpting of the wings by me was not only acceptable, but also a very necessary part of the process. Amazing!

Back view of Angel Doll ALCEE 'The Old Crone'

---

[3] The Wizard of Oz, written in 1900 by L. Frank Baum. Later a 1939 movie directed by Victor Lonzo Fleming and starring Judy Garland.

Next was the costume…those miniature costumes. I remembered Barbie Doll clothes, and how difficult they were to sew. My creations required somewhat larger costumes, but still proved challenging. I would secure a seamstress; after all sewing is what they do best.

There happened to be a seamstress living in my neighbourhood that made the most beautiful wedding dresses. Aha, perfect plan, yes, she would sew the costumes for me, and I would provide her with the ideas for style, fabric etc. Great idea, right? Wrong!

Somehow everything she created did not look or feel right. Then I went a step further and perused other angel designs and their costumes, but no…I was to produce these Angel Dolls entirely myself. Upon reflection, I came to thoroughly enjoy every stage of designing and creating these remarkable *Angel Guides*. "Guides" I believe to be the operative word.

A significant part of the process for me is the fascination with my hands and their ability to know exactly what is required. It is as if the Angels are creating themselves. They mould and manipulate my hands to do their bidding. "A little more here, a little less there, don't forget his dimple…her jaw is much stronger, and the forehead is wider than that." Each Angel Doll is unique unto themselves: every step of the process guided, from the skin tone, colour of eyes, and the textures and patterns of fabric.

Many times, throughout the early creations, I struggled while attempting to sculpt the hands equal in size and proportion; often giving up in frustration. "Oh, forget it, this'll have to be good enough!" Only to have the recipient later comment or ask, "How did you know that his finger was shaped like that?"

Repeatedly I was shown the discrepancies in my perception, and the futility of not surrendering to the will of the Angels. It was ultimately an exercise in trust and acceptance. Then there were times when I questioned whether my sanity was intact… as I sensed *issues* with the client or had an insight into a *specific time frame* of the individual. Sometimes I was transported

Angel Sculpture GHANDI

energetically to other *realms* and *dimensions*. Could I accept their sexual preferences, indeed their choices? Would I be truly willing to allow the *vibration* of the Angel creation to come forth? I remember the absolute fascination with the entire process.

Angel Sculpture GRIEBE

Many friends and family members wondered what I was doing communicating with Angels. Words of caution were often expressed from their fear of going beyond the 'norm'. These people are my Earth Angels, allowing me to see and sense my own fears of the expansion of love. I never cease to be thankful for the soul family that came forth during this time. We supported and continue to support each other in our choices to release, forgive, and surrender age-old belief systems individually and collectively.

There were to be many Angel Dolls created, and they would continue to teach me about colour, race, and creeds. The story I'm about to share with you helps me weave the tapestry of the Angel's message.

Sometime ago I created an Angel Doll by the name of JEREMIAH for a friend who was moving back east to Toronto. The Angel's skin tone was ebony. My heart sang with the *remembering* of this *Angel vibration* throughout the entire creative process. It occurred to me that JEREMIAH and I must have shared many *lifetimes* together for me to feel and sense his *vibration* so deeply. Further affirmation came directly from my grandson Joshua.

As it happened, my grandchildren were coming to stay with me for a few days to allow their parents a mini vacation. The children were young, and in their receptivity were very much in touch with the *energy* they detected in my workshop. My youngest grandson Joshua chose to share his knowledge of the *energy* of a black man that was standing in the doorway of my workshop. Joshua was uncertain about this man and what his intentions were for being there.

Angel Doll JEREMIAH

I immediately sensed what I perceived as fear from him. To alleviate any discomfort my grandson was experiencing, I explained to Joshua my understanding that no *energy* or *entity* can invade your personal space and that you may ask it to leave. I then checked in with Joshua to see if the *energy (the black man)* had left. "Yes," my grandson informed me, "the black man is now outside the house but tells me he will never leave me, Grandma."

It is with the Angel's message to Joshua that I begin to understand what is really transpiring. I am working with the *Angelic realm* here in my workshop so Joshua must be seeing an Angel. It now occurs to me to ask Joshua if this *energy (this Black man)* has been to visit him in the past.

"Oh yes," says Joshua. "When I'm in bed lying on my top bunk, I can see him as he dances on the roof tops."

It was then that I realized what Joshua was seeing was JEREMIAH, the Angel Doll I had sculpted. Joshua had seen only pictures of white Angels, so it never occurred to him that Angels, like people, come in many colours! Whom would he ask?

This experience was wonderful for my grandchildren and me on so many levels. We were able to open up a dialogue about these newly discovered insights. Angels present themselves to us as all colours, races, and creeds in exactly the manner we require. They also show us clearly the importance of trusting our feelings above everything else. Joshua knew this *energy* well. He had been comfortable with this black man in all his previous encounters. Yet when this same *energy* presented himself out of context Joshua became uncomfortable. Why? Because he had a belief that Angels were white.

He felt very comfortable with this black man…this *energy*, yet the moment Joshua intellectualized this *energy* to be something that was at odds with his fixed perception of Angels, he became fearful.

Trusting the feelings of comfort and joy that the Angel JEREMIAH provided for Joshua, was the only measurement required. That day, the Angels taught us a valuable lesson indeed.

The Angel Dolls came forth one by one. Through word-of-mouth advertising, new commissions presented themselves. As one *vibration* was complete, another would arrive. Some Angel Dolls came accompanied by a poem unique to the *vibration* of the individual…some short and others a message of considerable length. This never ceased to amaze me, because poetry was not something I liked in school. A

new language unfolded for me as I focused within these *frequencies*. I became comfortable in sharing what I sensed, and what I knew about all that was being communicated to me.

I have come to believe in the *divine* order of these *frequencies* and their purpose. The Angels have chosen to bless me with their presence. The recipients of these sculptures have found varying degrees of familiarity and deep-seeded connectedness. The Angels' dedication to humanity and their decision to honour my journey in this remarkable way remains a mystery for me.

Elsie

An ANGEL DOLL sculpture

Angel Doll Stories

As the director of your spiritual evolution, your guardian is the initiator of many challenges. Difficult times are a sign that she is hard at work, helping you to change. When behaviours or beliefs interfere with your next stage of development and you are unable to consciously release them, she helps you through any unpleasant and unwanted circumstances, easing your distress. Simply believe in the surety of her loving response as any doubts will block your ability to receive help. Think of your guardian as friend and companion rather than a lofty, unimaginably powerful being. She walks by your side, lovingly guiding and assisting you. She knows you so well that she is there for you, even before you think to call.

Angel Blessings[4]

---

[4] Angel Blessings Cards of Sacred guidance & inspiration by Kimberly Marooney; Fair Winds Press, 33 Commercial Street, Gloucester, Massachusetts

BUFFALO WOMAN

Angel of Healing

Angels Do The Darndest Things

Story by Jeanette, Cobourg, Ontario, Canada

I received my Angel Doll as a birthday gift. My nephew, who had carefully transported it from British Columbia, presented her to me. He informed me that my sister, Sandy, had asked him to personally transport the gift to ensure its safe delivery. His anticipation of my reaction was obvious. He repeatedly reassured me that, "You are just going to love this Aunt Jeanette…you are just going to be blown away!"

And I was! Imagine the normal excitement one feels when presented with a large present in the form of a box. As I carefully pulled away layer upon layer of paper and tissue my excitement mounted. I had absolutely no idea what "it" might be…but knowing my sister's reputation for giving the most amazing gifts, I was intrigued. Imagine my surprise and consternation when the present, unveiled, appeared to be a doll in buckskin, an angel in buckskin with a face that appeared to be laughing hysterically at me. I was literally at a loss for words as my nephew tried to explain that these Angel Dolls could be prayed to, looked to for guidance and comfort. I am sure that he thought I did not appreciate this wonderful gift. He could not possibly understand that my immediate reaction sprang from our early upbringing in the church and the passage, "…thou shalt not worship graven images…" I felt a mixture of awe, at the workmanship of the doll, and an underlying discomfort at having a graven image in my house permeating the patterns of our everyday lives. Consequently, the angel was positioned in the hallway with some other native artifacts. It was my intention that whenever someone walked by her, she would be glanced at and appreciated for her beauty or at least the craftsmanship. Certainly not for any angelic vibrations.

Over time funny things started to happen. One wing started to fall away. At about the same time the direction of my own life seemed to be constrained and disintegrating. No matter how much I tried to put the wing back on, bits of it kept breaking and my response was, "Of course you fool…the wing was fragile, and you weren't careful enough."

Then we moved. It was an acrimonious move. Angel girl was sitting on the stairs. I was hurriedly packing up last minute fragile items for, yet another move and I picked her up by the head, as my other hand was full. The head pulled off and the body fell, breaking off her left hand. I was devastated. It was a mirror of the way in which my whole life seemed to be disintegrating. I carefully picked up the pieces and stored her away until a safe place could be found.

Eventually she did find a safe refuge but by then her other wing was damaged not so unlike her owner. As I look at her today (I have brought her down to face me as I write this), she still has that slightly giddy look

Angel of Healing

about her. However, time seems to have etched a questioning, somewhat bemused expression, an undertone of sadness mixed with hope on her face. As she stands here, minus her left hand and only one wing, she seems to reflect that will to keep going…to not quit…to see her injured self like the character in Monty Python's Holy Grail as suffering: "Just a flesh wound, mate!"

Is this art reflecting life, the theme that has run like a constant thread throughout my life? I'll let you be the judge of that.

JARRIS
Aspect of Jesus

Aspect of Jesus

Story by Marydith, Grand-Bend, Oregon, USA

Seven years ago, Elsie gifted me with a sculpture of my Angel. It was male, with angular facial features, very long arms, and large, long-fingered hands. Though his face was unusual and distinctive, I was especially taken with his hands. They looked familiar to me…as though they belonged to someone very dear to me. A sense of love, longing, and even a knowing arose in me each time I looked at them.

Elsie's gift came at a time when I certainly <u>needed</u> an Angel! My 25-year-old son had recently died in an auto accident. He was my second son to pass away, and I was devastated. I grieved in the solitude of my high-mountain cabin…alone but for my Angel standing by, so tall and graceful, on my bedside table. Perhaps it was a result of my acute grief and loneliness, but as the months and years passed, there was a growing vibrancy in his large, warm eyes. Sometimes, I swear, I witnessed a sort of glow from his face. I marvelled that Elsie's hands could create such a life-like being with clay!

The years passed, and my days filled up with business, and I paid less attention to my Angel. Eventually, I moved to town and packed him lovingly and carefully away. My apartment was small and temporary. Why risk breaking him by unpacking and packing him yet again?

Another year passed and something wonderful happened. I fell in love and married a beautiful man named Jon. He soothed my hurting heart with his warmth and tenderness…made me laugh with his quick wit and humour…and awed me with his grace and integrity. I loved his hands!

My heart melted when he held my hands in his own…so large and long fingered that both of mine fit in *one* of his! These hands were so familiar to me…And then it dawned on me! Yes! "These were the hands of the Angel!" I said this aloud one night as we snuggled on the couch. Jon was puzzled and wanted an explanation. I told him the story of my Angel…not knowing what his response might be.

He jumped up and headed excitedly to the garage. "I've got to see this guy," he said. I joined him and we quickly recovered Angel Doll JARRIS from the myriad of stored boxes. Jon was amazed as he looked at Angel for the first time. "I see ME in this guy!" he said quietly. It was true! Not only were the <u>hands</u> Jon's, but the long arms too…and the crook in the nose, and the tall, graceful stance. All were mirrors of Jon!

But most impressive of all was the warm, vibrant look from Jon's eyes…the same look I'd recognized in my Angel's eyes all those lonely, grieving nights, alone in my mountain cabin. My Angel truly did come alive… in the form of my dear husband, Angel Jon…and the healing has been miraculous!

ROBERTA

Roberta

Story by Linda Penn, owner of Bear Creek Miniature Train, Surrey, BC, Canada

While I was shopping for Christmas gifts, I happened to meet a friend of mine, Shirley. She was sitting at a table in the mall waiting for her friend Elsie. As soon as I was introduced to Elsie, I liked her and felt as though we had always been friends. When I asked what she did, she told me she sculpted angels and agreed to provide me with a portfolio.

At the time my husband and I owned and operated a children's train in a local park. We were preparing our Christmas display, part of which included a 108-foot tunnel that we decorated seasonally. After perusing Elsie's portfolio of angels, I knew I wanted one for our Christmas tunnel display. I asked her if she made them life size. She said yes, and so I commissioned the birth of ROBERTA.

ROBERTA was a 6-foot-tall angel with magnificent wings, covered with long white feathers that filled the backdrop above her shoulders. ROBERTA'S dress looked like Disney's™ Cinderella[5] dress, with a wide pink and purple sequined skirt draped to the floor with flounces looped around it.

Other than her dress, there was nothing soft or cute about ROBERTA. She was a solid and powerful presence. Her nose was long and her jaw strong. Her cheekbones were high, and her features resembled the North American Indigenous person, with his pride and power chiselled into his cheeks, jaw, and forehead. Her hands were large and capable, more like a man's hands than a woman's.

This was an angel who could accomplish anything and wouldn't take no for an answer…she didn't have to. Roberta exuded confidence and you could see that anything she wanted could be accomplished; and she seemed to carry the knowledge of 'how.'

When I first saw her, all I could see was her beauty. Not the exterior beauty we think of today as represented in the fashion magazines. It was more a beauty of character, of inner strength and capability. She exuded it through every part of her being.

The children loved Roberta and often commented on her beautiful wings. They just saw her as an angel. It made angels real for them.

---

[5] An old fairytale thought to have originally been written in French by Charles Perrault in 1697.

Not everyone saw her beauty though! Apparently, some of the other people working on the train had a very negative reaction to her. One of the engineers nicknamed her Gaylord. The men seemed to hate her and called her ugly. One time when she was stored in our warehouse, they put a scarf around her head and a long black wig for a beard. They made snide remarks about her and her strength. It always made me curious as to what they were afraid of. Was it her power? She looked very powerful and capable. Perhaps she symbolised the power and capability of women in general, and this made them uncomfortable!

It also made me wonder if men are somehow afraid of a woman's power, and as a result find it necessary to make fun of it. In my experience of patriarchy, men oppressed women and made them 'little' by exerting power over them, and often withheld the things women needed most. Often men use physical and emotional abuse to control the very women they care about the most.

Do women do the same to men too, because we don't even recognize our power, or don't claim it? I have

Angel Sculpture ROBERTA next to a Christmas tree

often wondered why men and women feel the need to do this to one another. Maybe it's because they feel powerless, and therefore need to belittle someone else to gain an artificial sense of personal power? Is it the recognition by men of a woman's innate power that scares them? Perhaps as women, it is time that we allow ourselves our own power and not its interpretation by others!

I know I am a powerful woman and I choose to wield my power wisely, so that I do not undermine another human being, male or female. Thanks to ROBERTA'S presence, I was able to see the many facets of myself that she mirrored for me. I know she held a light in the tunnel, to show me my inner strength and power, and to hold that place for me until I could claim it. The Angel ROBERTA also taught me about allowing others to have a different perspective from mine.

What about my strength? Was I afraid to show it for fear of being made fun of? I was teased a lot for allowing the Angel ROBERTA to be in the tunnel and for having her created in the first place. Do I even understand how much power I have as a woman? And am I afraid of my own strength and power because it is huge? Questions, so much of my self-exploration only leads me to more questions.

Do I feel more powerful than my man, and do I not want to undermine him? So, do I hide my power, my knowing and my truth? Do I belittle him, so I feel stronger?

What if both of us were to be powerful at the same time, without diminishing each other in any way? What if we can allow our gifts to come forth? I have not actually seen a relationship like this and yet I know it is possible.

We have an interesting journey together in discovering how to honour one another and allow the full power of our being to shine through in equality. This is what I choose. A relationship where I can be who I am, and my partner can be who he is. Where we can both accept our personal power and use it wisely for the highest good of all. Strength and creativity are powerful forces in both of us. I now claim my power and choose to allow him his. Thank you, ROBERTA!

ANGEL OF PEACE

The Family Gathering – Bridging All Nations

Angel of Peace

Story by Julie, Sooke, Vancouver Island, BC, Canada

I received my Angel Doll ANGEL OF PEACE from my grandma, Elsie, for Christmas one year. My first impression was that the Angel had dark skin, like my own. Secondly, I noticed the colours that my Angel wore were turquoise and black…contrasting colours for sure!

Turquoise – peaceful. Black – commotion. Interesting indeed!

Looking back, now I can see that I was given my Angel Doll during a very confusing time: the teenage years…where everything and nothing made sense. It was kind of ironic, to be given a gift of Peace in the midst of the mind's storm.

To be quite honest, I never really thought of Angels as being as spiritual as some might think. Personally, I don't believe that Angels have anything to do with our prayers. I do, however, believe in Guardian Angels and if that is the vision that my grandma was given then that's what is!

It was a beautiful gift to bestow on me and I admire the talent of the craftsmanship. The ANGEL OF PEACE is something I will cherish forever.

This is a substituted photo for SERVRINA

SERVRINA

Angel of All Nations

Angel of All Nations

Story by Dana Lee-Anne, Vancouver, BC, Canada

My Angel Doll SERVRINA was a gift from my mother, Sandra. Mom had recently met a woman who sculpted Angel Dolls. The purpose of the creation was to assist an individual in establishing an intimate exchange with their Angels. Mom expressed her desire to introduce me to my angel so I would know there was always someone to watch over me and my twin boys.

Upon receipt of the commissioned sculpture, Elsie explained, "SERVRINA is to be a Guardian Angel Doll for Dana, and with time Dana's understanding of her will become clear." SERVRINA was dressed in a flowing pink gown, the ideal backdrop for her long dark hair and beautiful wings. In one hand she carries roses, representing the flowers from the Tree of Life. On the other hand, sits a dove. This dove reflects SERVRINA'S intention as an 'Angel of All Nations' here to serve humanity.

When I first received my Angel Doll, I wasn't quite sure what I thought of her looks. I do know that she didn't fit any perception of angels I had at the time. However, I did like having SERVRINA on my dresser where I could see her. Somehow, she provided me with a sense of comfort. I think it was the same for my two-year-old twins. They were certainly intrigued with their mother's Guardian Angel. Whenever they touched her or her gown it was always very gentle almost with reverence. Considering how young they were, it was quite remarkable.

One day my eldest, Myles, asked if he and his brother had a Guardian Angel of their own. I shared with him the explanation my mother gave me when I asked her the same question. "When children are born, their mother's guardian angel takes on the care of the children, until they reach an appropriate age or state of maturity." So SERVRINA was indeed their guardian angel, as well as Mommies. Myles appeared to find comfort in this.

The true test for believing in the existence of SERVRINA as my Guardian Angel was to happen under the most unlikely circumstances. It was Thanksgiving weekend in October and my birthday. Corey, the twins' dad, the boys, and I were all invited for dinner. My little family had recently moved to a suburb of Victoria called Cadboro Bay, on Vancouver Island. Corey's parents, who lived in Sidney, extended their dinner invitation to include my mother. When I called my mom in Vancouver to extend the dinner invitation, I asked her how to make her pumpkin-and-apple pies. I wanted to make a good impression with John and Penny, so I attempted two homemade pies as my contribution to dinner. They turned out great! I was very happy with myself.

Mom would arrive by ferry later in the afternoon. Meanwhile, Corey and I were hustling to get the twins ready and to pack up the car. When we were all set to go, I came out with the two pies on a cookie sheet, covered with tea towels…they were still warm from the oven. It was my intention to hold the pies on my lap for safe keeping while Corey drove.

To get to Sidney from our place, we had to take the highway. Shortly before arriving at the on-ramp Corey pulled into a Gas Station. While he ran into the store, I carefully opened the car door, got out, and placed the covered pies on the roof of the car; then grabbed the nozzle for the gas.

Once the gas tank was full and everyone settled back in their seats, we were on the road again. Almost immediately after accessing the highway a passing car started honking and waving like mad! Corey's immediate remarks, "The idiot honking at us is being a total jerk!" was certainly indicative of his rising frustration levels.

But onward we drove, with somewhat lame attempts to include the twins in playfulness. Corey redirected the conversation to my mother's anticipated arrival at the ferry terminal.

"Do you want me to pick your mom up at the ferry for you?" he asked.

"No, but thanks. She will be so excited to see the boys, I feel I should meet her myself and take the twins with me." That's when it hit me! "Oh my god!" I started to cry; I was bawling so hard I couldn't even answer Corey when he asked, "What happened? What's the matter?" All I could choke out was, "The pies, Mom's pies!" Sob, sob, sob.

As soon as Corey pieced together what had happened, he pulled the car over to the side of the road. Reluctantly, he climbed out to look.

"Dana," he said, "you need to get out of the car now!"

I did, and there on the roof of the car was the cookie sheet with two pies still covered with tea towels! At the same time Corey and I looked at the pies, then each other, and said, "Oh my God, Mom's Angels!"

I lifted the cookie sheet off the car roof and sat carefully back in my seat.

The whole experience was surreal! When we reached his parent's house, we told John and Penny what had just happened. John, being the pragmatist, said, "No, it just isn't possible. There is no way those pies stay on the roof of the car!" Penny, on the other hand, said exactly what we did. "Your Mom's Angels," and laughed with joy.

Later at the ferry, I told mom the story…the story of the pies, the cookie sheet and most incredible of all, the fact that even the tea towels were still covering them! We had truly defied natural laws! Best of all was the opportunity it gave me, Corey, and Penny, to experience the power of Mom's Angels first-hand! It was only after I'd finished the whole story that mom, with an enigmatic smile said, "No Dana, not my Angels! Your Guardian Angel, SERVRINA."

Group photo of Artimus, Arteous, Elcee & little ones

SURROUNDED!
An Angel Doll Experience

An Angel Doll Experience

Story by Billie, Hope, BC, Canada

I sit here at my computer and wonder if I can ever put into words the events of the 3 days surrounding the death of my nephew and how it pertains to Elsie's Angels.

I wake early, as I often do when I'm away from home. It's strange to be alone in Elsie's house, strange to rest my head on her pillow. Whose dreams are these anyway! I make a cup of tea as the phone rings; it's my husband Ernie, who always wakes early. He tells me Jamie, my younger sister's only son, has had a stroke or something undetermined that has rendered him unconscious and on Life-Support. He's a 25-year-old boy in excellent health! What has he gotten himself into?

I hung up the phone after planning to meet at the hospital later in the day. Again, the phone rings, it's Linda Penn. She tells me she has a bird in her house that she can't get out and asks me what I think it means. I don't know. This woman's *knowing* is so powerful, I'm surprised that she's asking me.

I tell her about Jamie, she tries to tune in on his condition but gets nothing; tries again, still can't make a connection, strange for this energy worker!

I sit holding my cup of tea, contemplating the gravity of these two phone calls that have arrived before seven o'clock on a Sunday morning and realise where I am sitting…in a chair surrounded by Elsie's Angel Dolls! They are before me, above me, and on both sides of me! At this moment they cradle and envelope my body in a warmth of peace I have never experienced. Even the air is sweet! My only thought is, "May the Angels attend you."

As the day progresses and my thoughts return to Jamie, the words "May the Angels attend you" repeat and calm me. Over the next three days as we learned that he had an aneurysm that quickly ended his young life, the Angels are ever present. I see and feel them around us.

In the five years since this event, these blessed angels have not left me. At any time as I go about my life, I can expect a soft voice to remind me to 'Allow'… "MAY THE ANGELS ATTEND YOU! MAY THE ANGELS ATTEND YOU!"

I now understand these beautiful angels to be mine, as well as Elsie's… yours too if you choose to allow.

I bless this dear woman for giving the angels a form that my mind's eye could accept until I was comfortable; and honour her for walking in her truth and light for the goodness of mankind. My eternal gratitude goes out to you Elsie!

ST. FRANCES OF ASSISI

St. Frances of Assisi

Story by Francis Patrick, Vancouver, BC, Canada

I chose to commission an Angel Doll from the mother of my children, Elsie, to assist me in developing a closer, more intimate relationship, to what I understand as SOURCE. Since receiving and coming to know the Angel Doll ST. FRANCIS OF ASSISI to be my guardian angel, this wonderful angel has brought to me a peace that I believe I would not have experienced otherwise. He also provided a newly found feeling of comfort within and around me that has enabled me to recognize and receive the love and support I have been in search of. With the development of my freshly acquired confidence came a realisation that many of the mindsets I carry are those of the Ego, and are no longer valid.

Initially upon receiving my Angel Doll, I realized that it met all my expectations. To me, the angel represents a spiritual symbol that is connected to the Holy Spirit. I have felt an immense gratitude and an expanded recognition of well-being since my Angel Doll became part of my physical world. The words from a song come drifting through my consciousness as I sit here recording my feelings… *'You lift me up where I belong'* – *Joe Cocker and Jennifer Warnes.*

Francis Patrick McGeough,
Elsie's husband and beloved father to Elsie's five children
July 8, 1940 – March 7, 2018

BARTHALAMEW

Angel of Discernment

Angel of Discernment

Story by Inga, Surrey, BC, Canada

Even as a child, I seemed to have been connected to the realm of the Angels, just by feeling, and I wouldn't have liked anything better than to live with them all the time. This indicates to me that there was a part of me that didn't want to come to Earth in the first place. As a grown-up, I knew that I was under their protection, and they demonstrated this to me by making sure that I did not get hurt in any way during war times in the 1940s. Even when the house next to ours in Germany was destroyed by a bomb; we all came out unscathed. I credited my Guardian Angel for this and have had a personal relationship with him ever since.

About ten years ago, my teacher Linda came into my life, and it has not been the same since. The Angels OPHILIUS, NEPHIOUS, and JEREMIAH seemed to have taken turns being around us during our study weekends, and our Workshops. One fine Sunday morning, Linda introduced me to the Angel BARTHALAMEW, who told her that he was going to be my personal 'Angel of Discernment.'

As you know, of course, our dear friend Elsie makes these beautiful Angel sculptures. The Angel Doll that Elsie made for me was the Angel BARTHALAMEW. He first showed up in my life *energetically*, for what I understood as the 'Joining of Mind and Heart with Source, into the Acceptance of Self.'

Elsie was able to make him visible for me and truly tangible in every way. I put my Angel Doll BARTHALAMEW, dressed in a silver mantle over a navy gown, wearing a scholar's cap on his ash blond hair, and holding the Sceptre of Wisdom in his right hand, in a central location where he was in my presence during my waking hours at home.

What a surprise it was for me when at our next session, Linda told me that my Angel BARTHALAMEW was saying to her that he didn't like being where he was; rather, he wanted to be closer to me, in my bedroom in fact! If there had been only a smidgen of doubt about the existence of angels, this request from my Angel Doll BARTHALAMEW certainly would have wiped it out.

That was about ten years ago; BARTHALAMEW stayed with me for a few years, and during this time, I was able to come to trust that Angels are always around me. They guide and protect me; no day goes by that my thanksgiving is not extended to them!

The invisible ones are connecting with me through my intuition and showing me their presence and support. These Angels guide and direct many aspects of my daily plans and decisions, ensuring that all turns out perfectly for the fulfilment of my life's purpose and its lessons. There are others in my life that I love: the people who, like the angels, are unafraid to display their genuine feelings of love and affection consistently through their caring. Earth Angels, I imagine.

Ingaborg Anna-Luise (Shulte) Shelton
August 16, 1923 – December 6, 2008

Born in Halle, Germany; Immigrated to Canada in 1954. Lived & worked in Kitimat, Montreal, Toronto, Vancouver, and finally, White Rock, BC. Survived by sister Eva in Sweden, and two nephews, Bernie and Gord. Brother Wolfgang passed March 23, 2009.
Inga met her bestfriend, Donna Herringer, in Toronto during the 1970s where both women were employed as buyers for Easton's. Inga soon became the much loved and adopted OMA (German for Grandmother) to Katharine Herringer, Donna's daughter.

Inga joined the angels in their realm on December 6, 2008. Not truly gone…and most certainly not forgotten…

AROMIUS DEMETRIOUS
My Special Angel

Angels Do The Darndest Things

Story by Willie, Langley, BC, Canada

In 1996, I commissioned my friend Elsie to create the amazing *Angel* she saw when she looked at me. Shortly after Elsie began sculpting her, my husband Jim and I went on a holiday to Mexico. During our vacation we entered a small shop with assorted Huichol Indian beadwork. The owner of the shop came up to us and said that he had been waiting for us to arrive. We were astonished as he began giving us several gifts to take with us.

A few days after we arrived back in Canada, we dropped in to see Elsie and my Angel Doll, DEMETRIOUS. She was beautifully done, and as I stood admiring her, Elsie asked, "What did you bring back for her?" I thought for a moment and suddenly remembered the gifts from the man in the store! The hawk feather and its message: "Life is the initiation... Right now a clue about the magic of life is being brought to you" was for DEMETRIOUS. The next day I took the feather to Elsie, and she quickly attached it to the angel's outstretched hand. It seemed as if my Angel Doll was reaching for it and was now complete.

When I first took her home, I was happy to have her as an ornament, but when I think back through the years, I have realized that my angel has always inspired me to create the wonderful life I live. She taught me how to believe in myself and others, trust, love, manifest and attract wealth and happiness. My life is full of abundance. I have a wonderful husband of 50 years, four beautiful children, ten wonderful grandchildren and 2 great-grand babies!

Every day I say, "Thank you." I know anything is available to us. All we must do is ask. I believe our angels are the guidance and strength that can change our lives. Thank you, Elsie, for creating my beautiful Angel Doll, DEMETRIOUS.

ATHENA
Angel of Love

Angels Do The Darndest Things

Story by Maureen, White Rock, BC, Canada

Angel ATHENA was an Angel Doll I received as a gift for my birthday. I was happy and very excited to receive her. It indicated that my mother, Elsie, was finally returning to her love of art. This appeared to be an important and necessary catalyst for her, after a lengthy absence of some five to eight years. My children and my husband believed this Angel Doll to be an especially nice and thoughtful gift for my mother to have created for our family…I am exceptionally proud of her.

The first observation I made about my Angel was her likeness, *not of me*, but rather of my mother. She does; however, appear to have my hair colour and blonde curls. This interesting Angel Doll is dressed imposingly, in a costume of sheer emerald green with satin fabric and a Celtic Plaid. I'm convinced the rich green material and Celtic Plaid reflects the Irish Heritage in my dad's lineage. When I look at my Angel Doll, I see both my parents and me. It is a gift from my mother that I'll always cherish.

One day this unique and wonderful gift will be passed on to a grandchild, with the hope that they, too, will pass it on to their child. What a beautiful birthday present from my mother; made just for me, a one-of-a-kind heirloom created with her beautiful hands. A true reflection of a mother's desire to share her love and protectiveness.

SELINA

Story by Linda Penn, White Rock, BC, Canada

SELINA was the name of the second Angel Doll I received. SELINA is an ageless woman who looks both old and youthful simultaneously. In her beautiful white hair, she wears one lone pink curl. It immediately reminded me of the old saying, "There once was a girl with a curl right in the middle of her forehead…" This amazing Angel Doll is dressed in a cheerful lime green skirt and a copper corset. SELINA has the most unusual wings…they are made from stained glass…and look more like the wings of a butterfly.

One thing that stands out the moment you feast your eyes on her is the fullness of grace and wisdom that she exudes! When I first saw my Angel Doll SELINA, I found it difficult to see the part of me that she had come into my life to bring forth…although I had no difficulty resonating with her energetically.

Three years were to pass before I completed my shift. It was at this time that Elsie noticed that I now wore a red curl in my hair, in the same spot as SELINA. I'm no longer in doubt as to the contribution that SELINA came forth to provide…and I can feel the shift in myself to a place of confidence and grace. I am much more understanding of my choices and accepting of myself.

In the physical manifestation of the Angel Doll, Elsie manages to bring forth a new part of the 'Self.' For me, once I was able to see that part, it was easier to accept myself fully and completely. I find Elsie's work to be healing and cutting-edge, as it continues to inspire me personally and professionally.

I have also created angels with Elsie in her clay workshops. Through a very easy process that she guides you through, Elsie brings forth the joy of creativity! A new acceptance of the creative aspects we all have inside ourselves was born during those workshops! Seeing the results of our beautiful masks and Angel Dolls enabled us to recognize that with our own hands we brought forth what was already in our hearts.

It was a joyful and fun experience even though the energy was often intense, as each person worked on different aspects of her art…and her healing.

Thank you, Elsie, for all your joy and creativity.

This is a substituted photo for Orania

ORANIA

Story by Arania Armstrong, Langley, BC, Canada

When Elsie first gave me my Angel Doll, I was so taken with the detail and effort that must have gone into it. I was also amazed at the Angel Doll's likeness of me. Some days I just fix my gaze on her dark hair, her teeth, or her ears. Other times it might be her hands, or the individual feathers on her wings. Of course, I always make it a priority to keep her close to me. She has a spot on my dresser, near my side of the bed. Every morning when I wake, there she is with her bright smiling face encouraging me to make the best and most of my days. As you know, this can be difficult to do with all the twists and turns of our lives.

When my children and grandchildren visit, they stop to look at her and say, "Your angel looks like she came from a storybook." So, I treat this opportunity as an opening to tell them little stories about my life when I was the same age as they are now.

Observing Angel ORANIA often conjures up memories of the time when I received her. A time that I will never forget because of the incredible enjoyment she truly provides in my life. I know that my personal angel story may not be that exciting…but, without a doubt, I would miss her very much if I did not have her.

SAINT PAUL
Angel of Wealth

Angels Do The Darndest Things

Story by Joan, Victoria, BC, Canada

Thank you, for reminding me of the gift of my Angel Doll, and of my intention to share the beauty of this Angel with others.

When I was presented with my commissioned Angel Doll from Elsie, what I saw instantly was his magnificence. I knew immediately that it was Gods' intention to share joy, majesty, wisdom, and wealth. One look at this majestic Angel and I could feel Gods' resonance in the fibre of my being!

I feel my heart bursting with song each time I observe the Angel Doll SAINT PAUL. It is his image of beauty, grace, and wellness that imprints his majesty upon my soul. I liken this impression to that of a smile…the kind that invades, not only your face but also your entire presence.

It is with *joy* that I share my experience of the Angel Doll SAINT PAUL with you. He instilled in me a desire for the *joy* that inner peace creates. May this gift he has blessed my life with become his gift to you also.

I have chosen to honour my personal Angel Doll by sharing him in the world. He has embraced me in the light of his love, the light of God. May his essence now embrace you.

SURVINA

Angel of Protection & Light

Angels Do The Darndest Things

Story by Ella, Brant, Alberta, Canada

Let me begin by explaining that my wonderful Angel Doll has been gifted to me by my dear sister and friend, Elsie. As her only sibling, I have been blessed to recognize her inherent artistic qualities for some time now. In fact, it was I who saw some salt dough figures being sold at an art show. Excitedly I called Elsie to share my thoughts on her ability to create her own style of sculptures. It was a direct result of this phone call that Elsie began making clowns for retail!

The thing that first caught my attention when I received my Angel Doll was her likeness of me. It was truly uncanny! When I sat down to admire this rather interesting sculpture, I was almost self-conscious. Her beautiful costume, the lushness of satin and the extravagant trimmings and adornments. Opulence discreetly understated. She provided me with a feeling of magic…a message perhaps, "Allowing one to be who one is, and to accept fully the privileges given."

My next observation was the Angel's stature, and the sensation of peace and love that seemed to permeate within and all around her. The angel's clear blue eyes, completely free of toxins, focused directly on the future…looking straight ahead. This Angel Doll was projecting an eminently natural sense of wisdom from aeons ago. As I studied this magnificent Angel it was as if she was beckoning me to call forward a *knowing*: "You can be free…simply by allowing yourself freedom."

I am so very grateful for my precious angel and the gift of love she represents. From the moment I received her, she has held a sacred space of honour on my bureau. From this vantage point she offers a constant reminder of her messages of Peace, Love, and Freedom.

The next Angel story I am about to share with you takes place in my home in Brant, Alberta. In my capacity as a registered nurse, I was offering home care to the gentleman in this story.

Angel Doll SURVINA
illuminated through beams of light

One morning at approximately 8:00 am, I went to my client's bedroom to get him up for breakfast. His name was Peter and boy was he excited over something he had just seen. Peter exclaimed, "I have just witnessed the most beautiful and spectacular stream of light. It came through the window blinds and shone directly on the Angel Doll sitting on top of the bureau. Only the light immediately surrounding the angel figure became brighter; it illuminated only the angel and nothing else around it on the bureau…how amazing!" he said.

There were Venetian blinds on the window, which were closed. It was not at all bright outside…and totally inconceivable that one stream of light would go completely across the room and focus only on the Angel Doll when there were other items around it.

When Peter shared his experience with me, I had no reason to doubt his vision. I immediately thought of Peter's wife, who was in hospital, and realized that she would be leaving us soon.

Approximately three days after Peter's vision, a phone call came, letting us know that Peter's wife was failing. Three more times she rallied. She was able to see all the members of her family, including a son from Vancouver. He stayed with his mother for two days…she was improving. He left for Vancouver only to come back two days later, for her funeral. A coincidence…I think not.

WHITE WOLF WOMAN

Angel of Forgiveness

Angel of Forgiveness

Story by Linda, Surrey, BC, Canada

The first Angel Doll creation that I received from Elsie was WHITE WOLF WOMAN. She was created in the image of an Indigenous person, a medicine woman with a walking stick, to assist me in walking my talk. WHITE WOLF WOMAN wore a beautiful buckskin outfit trimmed with intricate beadwork. She had long black hair that was braided, and elegant white-feathered wings. Her beauty was undeniable, yet I found myself angry and upset to see her wearing a rabbit fur cloak. In my belief system, rabbit means 'full of fear.' I was clearly of the opinion that WHITE WOLF WOMAN represented me, or at least some aspect of me. Therefore, I was concerned that the beautiful, wise, knowing woman inside of me was cloaked in fear.

On the other hand, my introduction to the WHITE WOLF aspect of me was very comforting. Through my knowledge of this animal's medicine being that of teacher, and WHITE representing sacredness, this angel creation seemed a perfect reflection of my journey. The solution for me was simple. I would just ask Elsie to remove the rabbit fur cloak. Much to my surprise and initial dismay Elsie's response was, "All is appropriate. This is what I was guided to place upon her and there is a reason for it." In that moment, it became crystal clear to me that I had to face the fact that my wisdom was cloaked in fear.

WHITE WOLF WOMAN sat on the mantle of my fireplace for over a year until Freedom, my Siamese cat, tore off the rabbit fur cloak and destroyed it. What I first witnessed upon returning home was the destruction wrought by my cat. As I investigated further, what became more important was the fact that the only thing damaged on the Angel Doll was the cloak…Wow. I knew at that moment with absolute certainty that I had successfully worked through my fear and had forgiven my choices. Now I was able to truly walk my talk. This was a powerful lesson and gift from a very wise teacher.

Angel Doll WHITE WOLF WOMAN
after the cat 'Freedom' tore off the cloak

NINALTO

Nina in the Tone of Love

Nina in the Tone of Love

Story by Nina, Comox, Vancouver Island, BC. Canada

I am happy to send along my comments and the *'knowing'* that I have experienced living with my beautiful angel for these past many years.

The name of my Angel Doll is NINALTO 'Nina in the Tone of Love'! What an amazing description of my magnificent Angel. For me she has become a most valued and treasured possession.

The Angel Doll NINALTO has always been positioned in the centre of my home, in clear view of the heart of where I gather with others…the living room. I have maintained this location of honour specifically for her regardless of what home I happen to be living in! What matters to me most is that she has a view for "overseeing" it all!

My Angel has been a tangible figure that has helped me on my journey to remember that we are not alone here on the earth – rather that there are energies present (that are sensed rather than seen) to comfort and assist us in opening our hearts to ourselves and others – being the love that we are.

I am grateful to Elsie for what she has created and chosen to share with me.

Blessings to you, dearest Elsie, and to you Sandra in what you are creating together!

HEATHER

Spirit Of Humanity

Spirit Of Humanity

Story by Elsie

Her gown of blue satin and underskirt of white silk
Radiate the energy of the creative Mother.
She holds the crystal in her right hand, the place of giving.
While in her left hand…the receiver, she holds a staff, adorned with the jewels of abundance.

The delicate seed pearls sewn patiently on the gown,
Activate a remembering of wisdom and intelligence
For the balance of all.
The gemstones glow forth, radiating the many facets
Of the knowledge of life.

The crown of gold, copper and silver represents
The balance of male and female energy,
Grounded within the human form on Earth.

From the spark of Light, all of life flows forth.
The source of creation, nourishing the life of spirit in Humanity,
Allowing the acceptance of Oneness within
Joy of Creativity – Love.

This precious Angel Doll was the last I created on commission…it was time.

Elsie

Back view of Angel Doll HEATHER

SUMMATION OF ANGEL DOLL STORIES

Elsie was determined to allow in place of her personal perception of Angels, a divinely inspired cornucopia of experience. The personal stories included in this book affirm Elsie's early recognition that trusting the Angels to guide and direct her creations was necessary. Not because of any personal understanding that she possessed, but rather through her willingness to offer the Angels a forum from which to communicate. The individual responses, and in some cases, reactions, carried the power of the Angels' messages out into the world in a way we could not have imagined! I am constantly reminded that the universe, which supports the sun and moon and all the stars in the heavens, is much better equipped to take care of the details of life than we are.

When the Angels asked Elsie for a true commitment to communicate God through her Angel Dolls, she said yes, simply with compliance. Elsie was able in that moment of truth to recognize her gifts, and her willingness to share them. Gratitude and honour were the only consideration. Each new commission inspired Elsie to greater heights of awareness and insight. Her talent had nothing to do with ego and everything to do with intuition. It was at this time that Elsie's *clairvoyance* and *clairsentience* truly emerged.

Elsie's Personal Angels

This message of healing is not subjective but rather collective. Angels are messengers from God. Your Angel Doll is but a symbol to realise Gods' Love and Joy within you always. In your Heart is a Sacred place, a Springboard of Joy; here is where your remembering of God springs forth...

Enjoy!
Elsie

ELCEE
Guardian Angel

Guardian Angel

Story by Elsie

This incredible Guardian Angel is statuesque in the flow of her off-white gown and soft auburn hair, styled in an intricate upsweep. Tilted toward God, her face is a composite of sheer joy and rapture. Seven miniature doves, white as freshly fallen snow, carry pink, turquoise, and maroon ribbons that flow through her delicate hands, and down around her gown. ELCEE'S large white feathery wings spread out in an embracing sweep, while in her left hand she holds a vivid crimson rose. For quite some time, the dove was always a symbol of my Angel Dolls.

The youthful and stately Angel Doll ELCEE was created to facilitate clients wanting the experience of creating their own Angel Doll. Although commissioned sculptures were costly, the most common reason for making the doll themselves was a desire to create their own design. Because of this, a way had to be developed to simplify the teaching of my art form.

I began by creating a basic format to provide an Angel Doll design that could be duplicated by others. It was important to use a minimum number of tools and to devise a costume without the need of a sewing machine; preferably with tools one can find in the average household. Wing construction was always taught in a separate class as wing creations are a delicate and lengthy process, for which there is no alternative.

The workshop participants took great joy and pride in what they were creating and in the choosing of eye colour, fabric, textures, adornments, and hair. I provided a variety of hairpieces; some synthetic and some lamb's wool, which I dyed in a variety of colours. On completion, these hairpieces were glued onto the doll's head.

It was fascinating to watch my clients place the hair. The actual change in the vibration of their Angel Doll was tangible…we could feel it!

Students were encouraged to contribute adornments which had special meaning for them, ultimately adding to the overall design. Often, friends and clients generously donated jewellery and other sundries for future creations. What a process…always perfection. As part of the materials for the workshop, I pre-made under-gowns, simple in style, as a foundation for the overall costume. One was made for each participating client.

For the Angel Doll ELCEE, a simple gown was made with one yard of 12-inch lace, which was wrapped around her arms, and over the under-gown, to create flow. A few hand stitches here and there, and her gown stayed in place. This design was easy to follow by practically anyone, making this type of format the perfect solution for my Angel Doll Workshops.

It was interesting during the step-by-step process to observe individuals being critical in their comments about how and what they were creating. It was often necessary to remind students not to judge the Angel Doll until it was completed. Ultimately, participants were happy with their endeavours and often amazed at their ability to tune in and allow their innate knowledge to flow naturally.

Often what they set out to create was nothing like the finished product. However, an overwhelming sense of gratitude permeated their entire experience and left them with a newly acquired respect for their intuition and the power of the creative flow. These workshops provided a safe environment to ask questions, and the opportunity for participants to share some of their life experiences.

ARTEOUS

Healing Angel

Story by Elsie

The Angel Doll ARTEOUS has one of the kindest and most gentle faces I have ever seen. He exudes *energy* of complete and unconditional support. He wears a simply cut gown of soft blue satin, highlighting his beautiful blue eyes. Flowing wings of white and gold fully embrace him. ARTEOUS holds delicate crystals in his left hand; the left side of our body represents our intuition.

The Angel ARTEOUS is an Angel that carries a vibration that is like the Angel OPHILIUS. It is my understanding that ARTEOUS came to assist me in the founding of the 'Joy of Creativity' Workshops. I designed these Workshops to enable students to sculpt their own Angel Doll. For the first year that I facilitated my Workshops, I was cognizant of ARTEOUS being present.

Design one was a small Angel approximately 8" tall. These sculptures were created with a ceramic-like product called Cernit or Super Sculpty. The student would sculpt the face and hands, then make an armature to fit over a base cone foundation. The garment was also of this product.

Design two was an Angel about 12" to 14" tall…same format of sculpting the caricature and armature, and then fitted onto a high-fired clay cone form. The Angel Doll was then dressed, with a simple gown sewn of the student's pattern, and adorned with whatever symbolism felt appropriate. With both designs, the symbols may have been a staff or crown, crystals, and semi-precious stones. Often, delicate quartz crystals were placed in specific chakras.[iii] Sometimes the students would share that the symbols they chose invoked a memory within them…a memory of the light and love that existed somewhere deep inside.

Students also shared an experience of release such as, "It is as if old mind-sets I've carried have been miraculously eliminated!"

In connection with the Healing Angel ARTEOUS, I remember a wonderful healing story. One day I was contacted by a newspaper journalist and she asked if she could interview me on 'my home-based businesses' of sculpting Angels. I agreed and invited her to conduct her interview while I was in the process of sculpting an Angel Doll. As it so happened, the Angel Doll that was on my work table at the time was the Angel ARTEOUS. This woman photographed me sculpting, while asking about my process. I simply shared with her what occurred during a workshop, or when working specifically on a commissioned Angel Doll.

Later, this article with the photograph of myself next to Angel ARTEOUS was printed in a local newspaper with the name of the journalist. Immediately after this publication I received a call from someone that knew me and was familiar with my work. This is where the story gets interesting…it turned out the journalist who interviewed me had a child from a previous marriage. After the break-up of that marriage, a new relationship developed for this journalist which seemed to create much contention between her child and the new partner. However, immediately following the interview, this relationship came to a more peaceful resolution. A coincidence perhaps? Or possibly the direct result of exposure to the incredible Healing Angel ARTEOUS…you decide!

Both during and after workshops, many stories were shared by participants about their healing experiences of hidden or subtle race discrimination, family hurts and circumstances, job-related issues, and much more. Quite often they would uncover a unique gift that came forth from their power of creativity…and the courage to pursue it. The understanding of the need to accept these gifts was a fundamental aspect of their healing; a truly necessary step in propelling the ripple effect of healing within their immediate families, and beyond.

Each time I hosted a Joy of Creativity Angel Workshop, I would make a completed Angel Doll myself. As such, I incurred a relatively large family. One of the personal Angel Dolls I created during a workshop was of a son that I had miscarried. Through this process, I was better able to get in touch with many unresolved feelings I had been carrying for a good deal of my life. As a mother, I finally began to recognize agreements that we make with other souls, and how important choice is for us all.

COYOTE MAN
Angel of Peace

Angel of Peace

Story by Elsie

As I start to sculpt a new angel creation, I feel a strong masculine energy. He has penetrating brown eyes, a broad forehead, and high cheekbones. His jutting chin is branded with a cleft; while his energy permeates mischievously, I can't help but wonder what's in store. His striking clothing consists of tan coloured buckskin adorned with colourful beadwork. Proudly he wears a long traditional headdress. I heard the name COYOTE MAN!

I assume this Angell Doll is for me, since currently I have no commissions. My inner voice, my *knowing* is very clear that Angel Doll COYOTE MAN will take me to new dimensions of creation!

Trusting in the process guided by the angels has always worked well for me. However, I sense a wariness about COYOTE MAN given my knowledge of 'Medicine Cards'. Coyote is trickster medicine and can be challenging to say the least. There is a tightness in my abdomen as I tune into my perception of this energy and my stomach clenches with fear.

I'm reminded of a statement I made to someone…Shift Shaper! "Don't you mean Shape Shifter?" was their response. "No, I think not. What I need now is to shift the energy within my mind, beliefs and perceptions before I can shape a new creation into my life."

I glean dimensions as colours of creation. I'm guided to delve into these vibrations. Sexual preferences and belief systems, man-made-laws, established without Truth! Yes, I know of these, but I'm still wary. I stay vigilant watching and waiting to see what the trickster is doing here in my life at this time.

Then it happens. One day, I'm returning home from work feeling very tired. I notice a fat mouse sitting in the corner of my front entryway. As I quickly rush past him to open the door, I can't help but observe how much this rodent resembles the plump little mouse from the story of Cinderella![6] I begin to wonder if my Neighbour is playing a joke on me. I even got closer to the mouse to see if it's real. Yes, most definitely! It does not appear to be leaving anytime soon so I go in. I quickly put the incident out of my mind until the next morning when I discovered him sitting in the middle of my driveway; just sitting there with his little whiskers twitching! Feeling generous I toss him some crumbs from my morning muffin and suggest that he might want to scoot…before the resident cats see him!

---

[6] An old fairytale thought to have originally been written in French by Charles Perrault in 1697.

Suddenly, I can hear my mother's voice: "When someone dreams of a rodent, it's a sure sign that bad luck is coming." So, this must be where my fear of mice and distaste of rats originated. As I enter my car, I can hear another familiar voice Angel OPHILIUS, "Well Elsie, old fears run deep!"

What? Could he be referring to the mouse? Then I'm consumed with another incident that had recently occurred. It was while my son's family was visiting. My grandson had come into the house after hurting his neck on my trampoline. "Can you fix my neck Grama?" he asked. His mother was sitting across from me, so naturally I asked her for permission to do so. After a noticeable hesitation she agreed.

I felt so hurt that she could think I would do anything that might harm my grandson or anyone for that matter. It was painfully clear now that my son and his wife harboured concerns about my beliefs and healing work. I was determined to proceed with the healing of my grandson's neck. Unfortunately, only a little release took place.

Because I had errands to run, I jumped in the car and headed out. While driving around I realized this unwelcome development with my grandson had left me confused and sad. Doing what I had come to do naturally, I asked for guidance. It was the energy of Jesus that spoke to me; assuring me that the situation is all in the communication. What my family required for its healing is for me to present a visual experience of energy work as light, in terms my daughter-in-law could identify with, like the light of Jesus, she would no longer be afraid: the work I facilitate is to assist clients in tapping into their pockets of fear. The purpose of identifying the fear is so it can be released, and the individual can experience a greater acceptance of this Christ energy. Yes, this sounds doable! When I returned home, I initiated a conversation with my grandson's mother. She and I were making headway, I could feel the shift…soon my grandson came in again and requested that I do more healing work on his neck. Receiving his mother's permission, he and I went downstairs to my treatment room. Very shortly his neck was fine and away he went to continue to play on the trampoline. Shift shaping? Yes, in my world.

At the time of this event, I was teaching healing art classes and workshops in my home. Shortly after this incident Angel Doll COYOTE MAN was sold to a brilliant soul, a young single mother and student. She expressed her desire to purchase COYOTE MAN because as she said, "I feel a powerful connection with his vibration."

ALCEE

The Old Crone – Sweeper of the Path

Angels Do The Darndest Things

Story by Elsie

My wonderful Angel Doll ALCEE is truly all-seeing, and timely for my life. Her sweet and kindly face is framed whimsically with flowing white hair. Large and fluffy wings are artfully tinged with blue, delicately encircling her satin gown. Handsewn seed pearls create a pattern of a multi-pointed star. At its centre is an aurora borealis stone.

As I sat patiently sewing these tiny seed pearls to the gown, I experienced old feelings and familiar images. Each generated physical and emotional discomfort for me. I became cognizant of perceptions of ageing that had not been conscious. "Old dried out female" was one that came up. "Women with warts, humped over canes, cackling, and muttering secretly!" Images that I held vividly, but from where? Books, perhaps?

Gradually as I finished sewing the individual pearls on this garment, all the uncomfortable memories faded completely! In place was a feeling of peace and admiration for the sacred wisdom of the "Old Crone." With genuine gratitude I give thanks for the opportunity to release my deeply embedded perceptions of the past. The grace of this wise and older woman provides me with a new perspective on the old crone!

A small diamond was carefully placed on the Angel Doll's throat *chakra*. On her head she supports a metal woven cone of copper, silver, and gold, shaped like a crown. Flowing from this crown is a long sheer veil, blue[7] in colour, enhanced by a sequence of pearls.

I was to understand that the metals were necessary in grounding Angel Doll ALCEE'S energy. She holds a brass staff that has a large synthetic diamond in her right hand. On her left hand she wears one continuous piece of jewellery; a bracelet designed of gold rings to represent the continuation of the cycle of life.

This creation assisted me in healing my discomfort of the label 'old crone.' She shared with me an understanding of the ancient rites-of-passage that are so necessary to a woman passing from one vibration to another. She was also able to assist me in recognizing, with honour and gratitude, how universal law is passed from generation to generation.

ALCEE 'The Old Crone,' now sits in a place of honour in my living room, overseeing all that passes through; and as I glance at her several times throughout the day, I am reminded of the gift of this sacred life. Visitors constantly tell me that there is an immediate feeling of comfort, and a sense of wellbeing that settles over them, whenever they enter my home. There's no doubt they are feeling her presence. In my humanness, I want to take total credit for their experiences; however, as much as I recognize myself to be an excellent hostess…ALCEE is truly the magic and love that permeates.

---

[7] Blue represents calm and trustworthiness.

JERRIS
Earth Guidance

Story by Elsie

The Angel Doll JERRIS projects a powerful energy that resonates from an ancient lineage, a source beyond time and space as we know it. I'm truly cognizant of Angel JERRIS whenever he enters a room because, like Jesus, a cold temperature invariably ensues! When I asked for guidance regarding the change in temperature being cold and very different from the other angel vibrations, I received the following explanation: "Due to the heightened vibration and frequency of Jesus–the master—it is necessary to reduce the body's physical temperature in preparation to receive!" I sculpted four variations of the Angel I call JERRIS. Three of the sculptures went to clients and one has stayed with me. As I sculpted this creation, I felt the presence of a tall stately being with flowing white hair. He is a wise and loving master, with beautiful blue eyes and a smiling face.

As always with these creations, the guidance I receive of colour and texture of fabric for the garment comes through. This Angel Doll's linen gown is simply cut with long wide sleeves and an even longer shawl of soft blue tones. Two five-pointed gold stars are sewn on the chest of his completed gown.

Whenever someone came into my workspace and saw him, they would inevitably comment on what a strong presence he portrayed. As one lady stated so boldly, "Whoever that dude is, I want that powerful energy with me!"

I have felt the vibration of the Angel JERRIS very strongly throughout my healing journey.

ANN

Angels Do The Darndest Things

Story by Elsie

The Angel Doll ANN was created in one of my Joy of Creativity Workshops. During her creation I began to recognize something very familiar about her, mother energy — yes — the energy of my mother Annie… how wonderful!

ANN was designed as youthful, innocent, and delicate. From her white gown and Angel wings there seemed to come forth an emanation of absolute purity of love. In her left hand she held a precious crimson rose… very much like my mother's favourite 'American Beauty' rose.

Since my mother had recently gone into a nursing home, the timing of ANN, the Angel Doll, was sheer perfection. I was quite confident that this Angel Doll would provide my mother with a great source of comfort. I took the Angel to the nursing home and placed her on a shelf in my mother's room, so that she might oversee all the comings and goings.

One day, each member of our family received a phone call. It was from a nurse that cared for my mother in the senior's home. She felt it would be wise for the family to come and say their good-byes, as Annie was soon to depart from this physical life. My mother was bedridden and was no longer able to speak aloud. My only sister Ella and all the grandchildren came, except for my daughter Angela, who lives in Australia. Each person shared some private time with Baba, allowing him or her to say their farewells, and to share their deepest, most personal feelings with her. Baba could have no doubt that she was well thought of and loved.

The time came for Ella and me to visit with her again. As the two of us sat next to the bed, one on either side of her, we shared with her all the customary statements of thanks and acknowledgements for all that she had given us. Then, as gently and lovingly as we could, we gave her our permission to pass over. It was our understanding that loved ones often sought permission to leave.

What happened next is a little hard to explain. My sister and I looked over at the Angel Doll ANN…she had a message for us, which was totally on a feeling level; it was this, "Your mother Annie, has already been given two windows of opportunity to pass over, but had declined them. There was still something that she wished her daughters to understand, more fully."

What she needed us to recognize was the importance of each generation, and its contribution. Every generation prepares the way for the next. The dedication of everyone to make choices in their generation ensures that same right for the next. It was Mom's intention to make us understand that she was passing the baton to us, in honour of her journey and in recognition of ours. As I sat contemplating the power of her message, I remember hearing and feeling with absolute clarity the following statement… "From her loins you were birthed, rejoice!"

Two weeks later, the Earth Angel Annie chose her third and final window of opportunity.

SUMMATION OF ELSIE'S PERSONAL ANGEL DOLL STORIES

"You, Elsie Mary, will make Angel Dolls. You will sculpt them and adorn them with magnificent wings and thought-provoking costumes. Through this process each Angel Doll you create will be aligning with their intended. This alignment awakens a remembering of the angelic realm in their personal lives. The guidance each Angel Doll provides will be as unique and individual as the recipients."

As I reread Elsie's message from the angels, I'm "gobsmacked!" A phrase I heard often from a dear friend of ours. In researching this English expression, I found the perfect description of my feelings…*overwhelmed with wonder!*

Elsie became the instrument of love required by the angels, through her willingness to align with the angels' message of love. Enabling the angels to provide a true expression of themselves in the world, ultimately an expression of God's love.

Who among us has not yearned for a connection, a confirmation if you will, that we are more? That the image that is reflected in our mirror is not the truth of us, it is simply a reflection? The true gift from Elsie is the opportunity to see ourselves differently. Each Angel Doll awakened something that was buried! A knowing, an understanding of perfection that was currently inaccessible to us.

Elsie is an instrument of magic! The magic that exists within each one of us. Her creative spirit aligned with her understanding of God and initiated possibilities "beyond her wildest imaginings." Each Angel Doll story offered in this book, reflects the generosity of the storyteller, and provides a unique opportunity for the reader to align with their intended!

What we as readers have gleaned from each story, is the synchronicity of universal timing. What is for us, what is needed, is here. Allowing is the key to unlocking the deeply entrenched perceptions that have distanced us from truth. "And so, the angels came to earth…to share tidings of peace and joy" …amazing!

ANGELS OF A DIFFERENT KIND

I would like to take this opportunity to thank everyone who graciously submitted their Angel Doll stories for publication in the previous section. Not all of these submissions could be included in this book due to the sheer volume of them, but it was humbling to see so many lives affected by the angels.

Speaking of angels, this seems an excellent place to pay tribute to Elsie's second husband Jules Poliquin…at Elsie's request. This beautiful man provided my friend with the love and joy she needed and deserved… **for it was he who expanded Elsie's heart and engraved his love on it for eternity.**

At this time, it seems somehow appropriate to include *Angel Stories* of a different kind. While these additional stories are not directly connected to Elsie's Angel Doll Sculptures, they have been submitted by caring individuals who desire all of us to benefit from their personal angel experience.

This desire to share has created an additional section to display more of Elsie's fascinating sculptures. As an introduction to each story tendered, we have provided the picture of a sculpture not previously provided to our readers. We hope you enjoy them as much as we do!

On behalf of Elsie, myself, and all the Blessed Angels that have guided our hearts, our hands, and our consciousness, *"Whatever the heart can feel, the mind can conceive."*

Because Angels live in our hearts.

Sandra

An ANGEL DOLL Sculpture

THE SHOPPING ANGEL

Angels Do The Darndest Things

Story by Dolores Wach, White Rock, BC, Canada

What! You have not heard of the Shopping Angel? Are you sure?

Recently, for our annual club picnic, it was my lot to devise a way to divide our membership into teams. I decided to have each person choose a slip of paper depicting an animal. As soon as they received the magic word that rhymes with "snow," they were to go milling about whilst emitting the sound made by their animal. Once they came upon another person making the same sound, they were to latch on to each other and see who else they could find making similar noises. That would become their team.

The animals I chose were cat, dog, sheep, rooster, cow, and pig. Rather than simply naming the animal on the slip of paper, I thought it would be more motivating to use stickers. Now I had cat stickers, sheep from the sheaf of nativity stickers and Snoopy to represent the dogs. Unfortunately, I had no roosters, cows, or pigs.

Hurriedly, I rummaged through my library for pictures I could simply photocopy and tape to the paper slips. Then armed with a card album (cow), an antique book (rooster) and "The Houghton Mifflin Dictionary" (pig), I headed to our town centre to use the photocopier. There is but one photocopy machine at our town centre. I could see it through the store window – OUT OF ORDER.

I returned everything to the car – even my purse – and walked dejectedly along the tiny strip mall heading nowhere in particular. I had run out of ideas and preparation time as well. I was sorely disappointed. In front of the photo shop I paused, and for no apparent reason opened the door and stepped in. There – right in front of me – stood a display rack brimming over with stickers, and there – looking me straight in the eye – were none other than a cow, a rooster, and a pig.

So now you, too, know – there is a Shopping Angel!

Beautiful Angel Doll Sculpture

ANGEL VISITATION

Angels Do The Darndest Things

Story by Aliyana Ruekberg, White Rock, BC, Canada

It was about 11:00am in the morning on December 24th, 1987. I was living on Long Island, N.Y. and driving in the neighbourhood where a dear friend who was also a therapist had lived.

Louise Rolfes had passed away from cancer the previous year in her thirties. Suddenly after just passing the street where I would have turned to go to her house, she appeared in the sky as an angel of light, huge and radiant. She was carrying a wand and wearing a long gown of shimmering fabric.

I felt myself being filled with so much love and this is the message she gave me: "Your father is ready to pass. We are preparing for and awaiting his arrival. All is taken care of. There is nothing to fear. Go to Toronto and be with him at this time. You will be carried and protected on your journey."

I felt at peace and calmly drove home and informed my son who was visiting that we were leaving the next morning for Toronto, a twelve-hour ride.

My beloved father, a wise and Orthodox Jew, passed away peacefully on the Sabbath, Saturday, December 26th, Boxing Day surrounded by his devoted wife, children, and grandchildren.

This is the only vision I can remember in my 68 years, and it will remain a precious gift for long as I live.

An Angel Doll Sculpture

THE SUNSHINE ANGEL

Angels Do The Darndest Things

Story by Sandra, Vancouver, BC, Canada

My story happened quite magically after a recent move to Vancouver, British Columbia. Not long after settling into my new city, I came across an ad in the newspaper. It was under 'Out of Town Real Estate.' As I read about 23 acres of waterfront property just beyond Mission, B.C., and the beautiful lodge style home, I was intrigued. I called the sister of one of my clients who was a realtor in Vancouver and asked her to arrange an appointment for me a.s.a.p.

She was pleased to accommodate me; however, it wasn't possible for her to join me this weekend. Would it be possible for me to reschedule at a later date?

Instinctively, I knew that I was to go immediately, and I shared this with her.

Heather, my client's sister, graciously arranged for the sales agent to meet me close to the highway to show me the way in. I thanked her and told her that if I were to purchase the property, she would receive her commission. What makes this story interesting is the fact that I was not in any position financially to purchase anything. Yet my intuition propelled me forward.

After a drive of an hour and a half, I reached the location where I was to meet the real estate agent. She was a wonderful young woman. At her suggestion I left my car and travelled with her to the property.

The place she took me to see was incredible! It was everything I had imagined for a Retreat Centre in a rural setting. As we looked through the house and talked about all its potential, something was nagging me. I couldn't put my finger on it. We left the house to walk the grounds with its ponds, waterfall, and stream. We admired the bird aviaries as we followed the path around this beautiful property, passing the neighbour's horses and barn. The agent and I were deep in conversation.

Now, as we talked, I could see *energetically*, a little girl about three years old. She was determined to get my attention. She started singing this song in my head making it very difficult to listen to the woman I was with. Finally, I stopped abruptly and told the woman what was taking place. When I informed her that the little girl was singing 'You Are My Sunshine' this poor young woman dropped to her knees, sobbing. When she calmed down, she asked how I knew her daughter. I explained that sometimes people talked to me in my head, often people I don't know or associate with in my life. They usually only do this when they have a message for a loved one.

The Sunshine Angel

The woman then asked me what message her daughter wanted to communicate. I shared the little girl's message in its entirety.

As we drove back to my car the woman shared with me the reason for her daughter's message, and how crucial the timing was.

It turned out that the little girl had died at the age of three and her favourite song was 'You Are My Sunshine.' Her mother had been remarried for ten years. Now her husband very much wanted them to have a child together. She had been adamant throughout their marriage that she just wasn't ready to replace her daughter. She had been praying for her daughter to let her know what to do, to give her a sign, a clear message that it was now time for another child.

The Angel, that little girl, chose me to deliver her message. She knew the best way to answer her mother's prayer, and I was honoured to serve.

An Angel Doll Sculpture

ANGEL ON MY BED

Angel On My Bed

Story by Adele Hooker (Mimi), Milwaukie, Oregon, USA

My husband received a call from his younger brother Bob. "Hey Bud, (his nickname for my husband Sam) our eighty-five-year-old sister Elna has been invited to play the piano for the 75th Jubilee of the Mountain Grove Camp Meeting. Your brother Joe, and I, want the three of us to go and surprise her with our attendance at the service! Do you think you can make it?"

So, Sam had an invitation to go back to those old familiar haunts where he looked forward to going every summer and spend a week with his friends. What a nostalgic time this would be and with three of his siblings, too. There will be just three brothers. No wives included. They'll have a ball. And I wouldn't put a stick in his way.

But I'm a scaredy-cat and Sam knows it. He doesn't want to leave me alone. He invites me to go along.

"Oh no, this is a stag party and I refuse to intrude."

"Perhaps you can get Katie next door to spend the nights with you? I'll gladly pay her."

"No, I'm a big girl and I don't want a babysitter. I've got to learn to stay alone."

"Then go stay with your sister in Seaside Oregon. She's just 85 miles from us and I know she'd love to have you play 'scrabble' with her," says Sam.

"No! I can't let fear drive me from my home. I have to face it sometime and now may be God's time for me to grow up."

"I don't think God cares if you go to your sister's house for a vacation," Sam salves my wounds. "And I don't have to go either. The boys can go alone, the two of them. That wouldn't bother me."

"Oh no, no. You're all in your seventies. They've both had open-heart surgery and nine bypasses, between them. This could be the last time you'll have the opportunity. I wouldn't forgive myself if you missed it to stay home with me."

And so, the time comes.

It's the night before Sam flies out at 7:55 am on Delta flight 878, breakfast included. I lie in bed awake next to sleeping Sam. I'm wrestling with my disturbing thoughts. I think of the basement window in the dark shadow of the driveway by the garage. I think of the ease with which serious intruders go through hidden windows and even sliding glass doors. We have two, one in my bedroom.

With my toe I reach over to feel Sam there. I wonder how I'll feel those ten nights when I can't touch him. I say a prayer for all those women who live lonely and alone. I've thought of them often and said an earnest prayer for them. Now I say one for myself. Then I hear these words in my mind, "Look. I have given you an angel."

I open my eyes and raise my head.

There she is, sitting on the foot of my bed, on Sam's side. She is shadowy, sitting sideways, facing toward me. Her left leg is tucked under her while her right leg hangs down off the bed. She sits quietly, without a word. But in her presence, all my fears drift away. I see them; two misty clouds float from me. I know their names. They are Fear and Loneliness. At that instance, I relax back on my pillow and fall asleep.

In the morning I wake. Not only is peace comfortingly mine but the angel vision is vividly with me. I can honestly say, "Honey, you go and have a wonderful time. Don't worry about me cause I'm not afraid, really, I am not!"

Small or big miracle, I haven't been afraid ever since.

An Angel Doll sculpture

HARLEY
Gift of Love

Angels Do The Darndest Things

Story by Adele Hooker (Mimi), Milwaukie, Oregon, USA

First, I should tell you about Harley. He is a big, beautiful, orange short haired cat. He belongs to our neighbour lady but comes to our house and stays all the time, day, and night. The neighbour lady says that's fine. Harley loves my husband Sam. But he gets romantic about me, sits on my lap, puts his head on my breast, reaches his soft paw up to lay it on my cheek and purrs.

He gets in the most adorable positions, lays on his back and stretches all four paws up with a soft white belly exposed. He curls his paws around his face and looks out from under them like a peek-a-boo baby; stretches out to touch both Sam and me when we take our nap.

He's so delightful we can't help but love him dearly. And he's so funny we laugh at him all day long. What a joy! We are always remarking how unlike an ordinary cat he is.

Next, I should tell you about my two grandsons who are in heaven. Their names are Eric and Joshua. Eric drowned at twenty-two months old, and Joshua died at the age of twenty-five in a car accident.

Now what I am going to relate to you will provoke a response of some kind, depending on how firm or flexible you are in your preconceived beliefs. All I can say is, I experienced this scenario. You can accept or reject it. I have no interest in the way you respond. That is your choice. I simply relate what I experienced.

A Happy Group of Sculpted Angel Dolls

This particular morning, I had just made my bed and was standing next to it. On my left side, *Joshua* appeared. Then on my right appeared *Eric*. In a few seconds *Jesus* appeared in front of me. This formed a circle, *Joshua* said.
Joshua shouted, "Group hug!" And we all had a warm, loving hug.

Then Harley came bounding down from above, into the middle of our circle. *Joshua*, smiling big, and in a happy voice said, *"Gift of love for your joy and laughter."*

Just a few seconds more and I was standing alone again. But oh! Oh! Oh! The joy of this encounter has not left me. How true! How true! My beloved ones and Jesus are here to bless me and are closer than I think.

And this adorable cat! He gives us oh, so much joy. He's a circus of laughter. A *gift of love* indeed! An angel of joy and laughter sent from my heavenly *angels*.

Love and Blessings,
Mimi

Little Nina Sculpture

THE EARTH ANGEL

The Earth Angel

Story by Karen, White Rock, BC, Canada

I have many angels in my life. God put those angels on earth to look after us in times of joy and need.

I met an amazing 'Earth Angel' back in 2001 when the world was in turmoil after the events of 9/11. Her name was Maureen. She had a small aromatherapy store in the area where I lived and every day, she would put her sandwich board sign outside the store.

The sign read: *10 Minute Chair Massage $10.00*

I passed by this store almost daily, going about my life and holding on to all the stresses that came with it. I used to read that sign and make excuses about how I didn't have the time to sit for 10 minutes, to benefit myself.

But one month after 9/11 had 'struck the world in the heart,' I was coming home from work and the stress of that day, and all the other situations that were going on in my life, all came to a head…and my neck was feeling <u>very sore</u>; over all I was feeling really low.

I pulled the car over to the curb and thought, *I need those 10 minutes right now. I believe this will help.*

I walked into this tiny shop, and there was the smiling face of Maureen, my angel. She greeted me with a warm welcome and immediately I explained in short that I wanted to try the massage. She sat me down on the 'Sit-aje-Chair,' got me comfortable, and applied some essential oil of orange. She also applied other special oils that she prepared based on how she was sensing the energy around me, and began her magical work.

Well, half an hour later the pain subsided in my neck. She offered me the bottle of oil that she had been rubbing on me and explained that the orange oil was the important essential that I should apply every day as it is an oil that wraps itself around the person and takes care of their needs. In other words, this was a natural antidepressant, just what I needed.

Maureen had only just met me that day, but it felt like she had known me forever! She also made me a special blend of oils and cream, just for me. My first thought was that I would apply those oils on my son who was going through the after-effects of a brain injury that occurred in a car accident two years before.

At the time, my biological mother, whom I had met four years before, was now dying of leukaemia. In her last three days of life while lying in a hospital bed, still conscious, my sister and I went to visit with her. We discovered my mother was feeling agitated from the effects of the illness. While I was sitting at the edge of her bed, I asked her if she would like a foot rub. She said, "Yes." As I pulled back the sheets it suddenly hit me that I still had those two bottles with the specially blended oils and cream in my purse!

I had not removed them from my purse since being in Maureen's shop three months earlier. I pulled them out, dabbed some oil on her feet and started to rub gently. The beautiful scent from the oils filled the room. For the first time since my mom had been in hospital, she was relaxed and sighing with a smile on her face.

Although I had bought my mom a gift certificate for a pedicure as a Christmas present, she had never had a pedicure or even a foot massage ever, in her lifetime…at least not until that day in the hospital. That blend of oils had an effect on my mom as well as the nurses who entered the room that night.

The next day, my biological mother went into a coma and died later that night.

Seven years have gone by, and Maureen is by far my most 'angelic' angel. We have been through many experiences together as women in business and friendship. This woman knows when I need a massage and when I need to talk. She puts the people she cares for first in her life, above herself.

She owns a bigger aromatherapy shop now and I run my own business. Maureen has been there whenever I need advice or just a friend to chat with.

Who is your Earth Angel? Are you an angel to someone you know?

The back of an Angel Doll

PHILADELPHIA CREAM CHEESE ANGEL

Story by Louise R., White Rock, BC, Canada

It gives me pleasure to recite my angel story to my friend Elsie…

I've never doubted the existence of angels, but my motivation in sharing my experience in her book comes from a desire to avail others of the enormity of angelic involvement in my personal life.

My story begins with a long-term illness not readily diagnosed and the frustration and fear suffered by me and my family members. The chronic nature of this condition led a hospital in Surrey, B.C. to refuse me medical attention, requiring my husband to seek help elsewhere.

I find the sequence of events a very important part of my adventure. The doctor at the next hospital, in Abbotsford, without ever having laid eyes on me before, suspected meningitis. TB Meningitis!

Devastated, my husband and I returned home to contemplate the possible gravity of my situation. The following day, my husband and our eldest daughter, Joanne, went back to the Abbotsford Hospital to see if there was anything that could be done. Upon my husband's return visit, the doctor was most apologetic as he explained that the only hospital equipped to evaluate my condition more thoroughly would be the Royal Columbia Hospital in New Westminster, B.C.

So it was that I went there.

It was December 8th, 1987; I was beginning to doubt that I would ever see another Christmas, my home, or even my daughter's birthday on the 13th of December.

Upon our arrival at the Royal Columbia Hospital, we discovered that due to the festive season a lot of the staff was attending their annual Christmas party.

The neurologist that attended to me on my arrival chose to interrupt the festivities by calling on the technician in charge of medical systems for the hospital. It was she that decided to leave the party to come and check me out and see just what this was. Later, a spinal tap was performed, and the earlier diagnosis of TB Meningitis was confirmed.

Philadelphia Cream Cheese Angel

My condition worsened…I experienced repeated seizures, several strokes, and for three months lay in a coma. The neurologist that had admitted me did not want me to have surgery. He wanted me to come out of the coma on my own.

As it turned out, my doctor went on vacation. In the interim another neurologist was put in charge. The following morning, he telephoned my husband to come into the hospital right away to sign papers for surgery. This neurosurgeon and another neurologist performed the necessary operation. This was when the first of several shunts were put in. After this surgery in March, I came out of the coma!

One day shortly after my operation, I had the most amazing experience which I hope never to forget!

It happened while I was sleeping. I found myself going through this long dark tunnel. As I was travelling through it, I remember thinking, "Where am I?" While I was still trying to figure this out, I came to the end of the tunnel; waiting for me there were three of the brightest Angels…all in white, with wings. The Angel in the centre was taller and they all appeared to be feminine. It was truly a sight to behold! (Every time I see those angels on television eating Philadelphia Cream Cheese, it reminds me of my experience.)

In my heart I could feel the message they came to give me: *"It was not my time to go."*

I'm not certain how many days after my surgery this visitation took place, what I do know is that it was a forerunner of things that were going to take place. I've always believed things happen for a reason and throughout this ordeal, I certainly met a lot of wonderful people. In all honesty though, I would prefer *not* to have lived the experience.

You know there are still days when I wake up and can't believe that I'm alive! I've never been able to figure out how I came to contract TB Meningitis. I do know that TB was something we could contract at school, but who really knows for certain, except for God. Just as He knew I would live!

Another interesting memory I have is of being regularly weighed throughout my procedure. The nurses weighed me daily when I was in the coma…one particular day I was aware of them when they came in and their intention to weigh me…immediately I became afraid of being dropped!

One nurse picked me up by the shoulders and another by my feet. As they were swinging me around, I remember feeling petrified…so much for a person in a coma not knowing what's going on. They took me to the scale and weighed me. I was shocked to hear one of them say, "72 pounds today." I'll never forget this *as long as I live*. Eventually the time came for my first visit home. It was now April 1988 and by May, I was allowed to go home for two days to see how well I could manage. I was on a lot of different medications for seizures, strokes, and TB Meningitis. I was to remain on the medication specific to Meningitis for another two years.

Time passed and finally by June 30th, 1988, I was discharged from the hospital. Gradually things began to improve to the point of me feeling like a living human being again.

This nightmare took place over 20 years ago and since that time there have been many more close calls! Times when my family were told to come quickly if they wanted to see me before I died. Times when, upon arrival, they discovered I had already been moved to the death room! But *no*…God and the Angels had other plans for me. What was the angels' message that day? Right: "It's not your time."

SUMMATION OF THE ANGEL STORIES SUBMITTED

The angels guide and assist our earthly sojourn as these stories clearly attest. Through these narratives, it becomes apparent that the angels choose the means available to answer our prayers.

Allowing is key! Trusting is the only viable language. Pleading and ringing our hands in despair, crying out in silence with the thunder and rumbling of an aching heart, or perhaps just a quiet and gentle whisper… this language is all too familiar. The angels hear our words, and at times the desperation that forms our communication.

I believe that each of us in our own way must find the path that leads home. Perhaps the purpose, the true 'Gift' from Elsie's Angel Dolls… "is beyond our wildest imaginings!" Whatever the intention, these angels assist in navigating this road. A remembering of the sacred is essential to trusting in God's plan.… remembering always, that each of us is *but a wave in the ocean of God*.

BARULIOUS

Sweeper of the Path

Angels Do The Darndest Things

Story by Sandra, Shaughnessy, BC, Canada

BARULIOUS, BARULIOUS, BARULIOUS where do I begin my experience of you?

You were certainly my first! The first physical representation of an angel, sculpted specifically for me.

Our Elsie approached me with a request for Inner Child sessions, which I was currently providing through private practice. Would I be willing to exchange a few sessions for a personally sculpted Angel Doll? "Absolutely, I would be happy and honoured to do so."

Alas…the introduction! You, dearest BARULIOUS, were dressed in the finest damask robe, topped by a vibrant blue silk cloak. I stood in awe of the size and detail of your wings and was genuinely intrigued with the ornate key suspended from a gold chain around your neck. In your right hand you carried a long staff, adorned with a magnificent quartz crystal in the shape of a hexagon.

The meaning of a staff, adorned with this important crystal, and its desire to prepare the path I would walk, was best researched. And so it is that I turned to a reference book for better understanding…

> "Quartz is said to bring the energy of the stars into the soul. Traditionally, the natural quartz crystal was said to both harmonise and align human energies – thoughts, consciousness, emotions – with the energies of the universe and to make these greater energies available to humanity. The natural tendency of quartz is for harmony, and it is recognized as a 'Stone of Power.' The quartz crystal can be used to facilitate both speaking with, and receiving information from, the spiritual and other-worldly masters, teachers, and healers."[8]

Wow! How interesting! And this key? What of it?

I'm reminded of a dream that is unlike any I've had before. I'm wearing a dress with pockets on the front. Intuitively, I reach into my pocket with my left hand. What I find is a metal key that appears old and tarnished. Carefully, I turn it over in my hand. I like the weight of it, and how it feels. Then it's time to return the key to my pocket.

---

[8] Book name is "Love is the Earth, a Kaleidoscope of Crystals" Updated-by Melody.

Sweeper of the Path

Next, I'm guided to a massive Cedar tree that displays an uncommonly large hole. "Put your hand inside the hole and pull out what you find" says a comforting voice.

As I reach into the trunk of the tree, I notice that I'm using both hands. What I find and lift out is another key! Very large, and ornately carved from wood. Considering its size, it is exceptionally lightweight. Not what I anticipated at all.

The memory of this dream brought forth the significance of the key the Angel Doll BARULIOUS wears! There is purpose in the 'Sweeper of the Path' bringing me the key from my dream. I'm still learning to intuit the key and its meaning…only thanks to him…I know that it is necessary for me to accept the gift of my keys, in whatever form they are presented.

Elsie in her wisdom, listened to and followed the angel's guidance in suggesting the exchange in services. Not only did I get to share my knowledge of the Inner Child, but I was also privileged to share the tools required to do so. The key the Angel Doll BARULIOUS brought was the key to unlocking our ability to receive. This can only happen when safety and trust are established. The Inner Child, the orphan, held the key.

The key the Angel Doll BARULIOUS carried for me was to change over time, as would my understanding of it. However, one thing was crystal clear; my angel had arrived, and I had been willing to receive. Thanks to my previous exposure to the angel OPHILIUS, I was open and receptive to my beautiful angel BARULIOUS.

My Angel Doll was given a place of honour in my living room where I found joy and comfort in his presence. The 'Sweeper of the Path' was truly responsible for preparing the way of a new and unexplored pathway. Sometimes it could be the path of least resistance…but not always. My opposition would often rear its ugly head and the challenges would mount. No matter what I created or why, the one consistency was the loving support I always felt from BARULIOUS.

WHITE ELK

Bringer of Vision

Bringer of Vision

Story by Sandra, Vancouver, BC, Canada

WHITE ELK speaks indirectly to my Mi'kmaq[iv] heritage…during a sweat lodge ceremony I attended during Christmas of 1992, her presence was made known to me, although at that time I was not privy to her name. I came to understand that we shared an affinity with vision through our ancestral predisposition as 'the green-eyed ones.'

Her long raven-black hair, and her tall, erect statute were not a physical trait we shared! Though we both have a tiny nose, ears, and mouth! I can't say that I ever saw myself in her; rather, what I perceived was a true sense of the sacred. In our early years together, I often felt her presence in ceremonies. She was also with me when I opened a healing centre in the Toronto Beaches — The Womans' Lodge: A Pathway to Healing for All.

The Angel Doll WHITE ELK stood in a place of honour in the Gathering Room at the lodge. Here, visitors and members alike benefitted from the amazing energy emitted through WHITE ELK'S presence. Beautiful wings dripping with soft, snow-white feathers. Her costume, a white buckskin dress with red beading stitched on the sleeves, the neckline, and around the bottom of her dress. Over her right shoulder she also carries a delicate medicine bag detailed with an intricate beaded design. Inside the bag is a tiny quartz crystal, a prelude I surmise, of the giant quartz crystal that graced the floor of this gathering space…

I'm now convinced that the personal vibration received from each Angel Doll, whether by gift or commission, was building a collective vibration that changed personal frequencies. Each time we willingly accepted and allowed the possibility that there is more in life than just the tangible physical manifestations that we've been exposed to, we began perceiving through other senses…*Clairvoyance* and *clairsentience* for example!

The more comfortable I became with my Angel Dolls, a new sense of comfort began to permeate the whole of my life. When I consciously chose to converse with angels, it became more natural to accept what I knew to be true. The more interactive I became the more enlightened I felt. Is it possible that all my angels are mirroring aspects of the divine that resides in me? Could be. Perhaps the angels are asking us to allow the mirror of the divine, which they have come to represent in the world, to reflect our own divinity.

NEPHIOUS

NEPHIOUS

Story by Sandra, Vancouver, BC, Canada

I feel compelled to write about Angel Doll NEPHIOUS, another sculpture created by Elsie and gifted to our teacher. Over these many years, I have been blessed to share a wonderful and fulfilling relationship with NEPHIOUS. He and Angel Doll OPHILIUS, often appear together. Although both of these angels emanate a profound and similar energy, their vibrations are distinctly different.

My reaction to this incredible duo is immediate! My entire body lights up with a smile that is totally uncontrived and bursting with joy! I'm convinced that the angels themselves see this state of being as an ideal condition for life.

As I reflect on Elsie's sculpting process for this Angel Doll, I would be remiss if I did not disclose the challenges; for there were many! Daily, she faced barriers that forced her to question her current beliefs and what she had come to understand about humanity as a whole!

One day after throwing her arms in the air in frustration, Elsie called me. With genuine concern she explained feeling lost and unable to hear or receive the angel's guidance…her concern was palatable. She then went a step further and asked me what I knew about the Angel Doll she was currently working on. So, without hesitation I quieted my mind and listened…

"Hmm…he is quite dfferent from any of the other Angel Dolls you have sculpted!"

"How exactly is he different?" asked Elsie.

"Well first, he has absolutely no hair…he's never had any. Secondly, he doesn't have ears."

"Oh, for heaven's sake!" she exclaimed. "This explains why I'm not having any success making his ears."

"Elsie, what I can tell you about this Angel Doll is simply this: he is otherworldly, physically different from anything we know, and he is here to challenge our perceptions."

Angel Doll NEPHIOUS certainly challenged me to revisit the deeply buried places within my psyche, where I coveted beliefs and perceptions that were at odds with my current reality. He provided me with a true sense of safety, the necessary condition for trust. Once trust was established, I could embrace the strength and courage to access these hidden crypts…these internal catacombs.

CONCLUSION

As the author of this book, I am choosing to end my contribution of personal Angel Doll stories here. As you can see I, too, have had many angel experiences throughout my long and lasting friendship with Elsie. I have been blessed in establishing lifetime relationships with WHITE ELK, JEREMIAH, OPHILIUS, and dearest ST. FRANCIS XAVIER, just to name a few!

These unique exchanges propelled my life into a formidable initiation of universal law and how it operates. Clairvoyance and clairsentience developed as muscles that I became comfortable flexing in my personal life, and in my profession as a counsellor and Reiki Master. As much as I would enjoy sharing more of my personal angel encounters, I'm convinced it would require the writing of yet another book!

Elsie and her merry band of women were determined to share these messages of love and faith, joy and laughter…even pain and sorrow. Through the angel's unorthodox methodology, many people developed relationships with their own divinity and recognized a true affinity with the healing process, individually and collectively.

The result of allowing the Angel Doll they received, either by commission or as a gift, to become a manifestation, a physical presence – even at the cost of long held beliefs and perceptions, as shared below by Jeanette, supports Elsie's intention to align with that of the angels:

"I was literally at a loss for words as my nephew tried to explain that these Angel Dolls could be prayed to and looked to for guidance and comfort…...he could not possibly understand that my immediate reaction sprang from our early upbringing in the church and the passage …thou shalt not worship graven images…"[9]

Elsie's contribution of a physical manifestation of our angels so that we were able to relate on a more personal level was a true alliance. She understood that humanity was best served with a hands-on approach to *divinity*, and that the *divine* aspect of angels lives within all of us.

Her bravery enabled many of us to re-establish *our* forgotten, but not lost, relationship of intimacy and respect with the angels. I know I speak now for my friend in extending our blessings to every reader who finds their way to these words. May they assist you in opening to the remembering of the angel you are.

---

[9] Taken from the BUFFALO WOMAN Angel Doll story on page 22.

GLOSSARY

* See endnotes for a more thorough explanation

Age-old belief systems: Belief systems that are passed on in the physical and etheric body memories and mentally through the unconcious. Often these beliefs are shared subliminally through generations.

Akashic Records: In the religion of theosophy and the philosophical school called anthroposophy, the Akashic records are a compendium of all universal events, thoughts, words, intent ever to have accrued in the past, present, or future in terms of all entities and life forms, not just human. [wikipedia.org]

Aligned: Adjusted to, in tune with, to be in sync with vibrationally.

Angel: A Being of Light – with or without body form. A spiritual being. Messengers of God; conveying the love & wisdom of the Eternal through them and transmitting that power to Heal and assist.

Angel Doll: Dolls sculpted – designed & created by Elsie Poliquin to represent the unique vibration of a specific angel - guide or soul.

Angel Guides: *See Angel explanation* -which provides guidance & direction in our lives.

Angelic Realm: The domain of Light Beings we understand to be angels…otherworldly.

Angel-Self: The individual Being of Light, of Spirit that you are.

Angel Vibration: The unique resonance of each angel which allows them to be felt and recognized.

Angelic Frequency: A Light Force vibration, a frequency that is increased or decreased – like the wattage of a light bulb - an identifier.

Aura: Coloured energy that surrounds every living thing; radiating colours that effectively communicate information about health. Emotional, physical, and spiritual.

*Chakra: Our etheric bodies contain major energy centres, located along an axis parallel to the spinal column of the physical body. These centres are called chakras, which means wheel or vortex.

Christ Energy: The frequency/vibration of Jesus Christ, Jesus of Nazareth.

Clairsentience: When broken down to its base components, it means 'clear – feeling'. Generally, when a person is clairsentient, their psychic information comes to them via feeling or sensing. Clairsentience is the ability to sense the subtle energies that surround you, as if the environment and people you encounter are sending secret energetic transmissions.

Clairvoyance: The ability to tap into; to see with the power of the mind; past, present, future events existing or happening out of sight.

Density: Compacted energy. All energy vibrates. The lower the vibration, the more density there is within the form. The higher the vibration, the more expansive the energy within the form.
Dimensions: Other worlds; often inaccessible, limited by our ability or willingness to feel or know.
Divine: That which is considered God or Universal Source.
Divine Inspiration: the process of having one's mind or creative abilities stimulated; of, from or like God
Divinity: The experience of the sacred

Earth Angels: The intention by a human, either conscious or unconscious, to execute behaviours that are for the highest good of all.
*Energy: [physics] the ability of matter or radiation to do work because of its motion, its mass, or its electric charge. Currents of life force.
*Energy Field: Serves as a container to hold & maintain the energy of the physical body. All life forms are composed of energy, which either builds matter or exists in a non-material form. *Addressed in endnotes under energy*
Energetic tablework: Working with a client's energy field for healing and alignment. Often performed while the individual is laying on a massage table.
Energies: A collective group of Light Force currants.
Entity: A thing of distinct and independent existence.
Expansion of Love: To intend love exponentially through light frequency.

Frequencies: The rate at which a sound wave or radio wave vibrates. The rate at which an individual, an animal, mammal, plant, rock, human being etc. vibrates

Giver of Gifts: The name or title the angels gave Elsie because of her ability to follow their guidance in creating Angel Dolls in an individual's personal frequency and vibration.
Guardian Angel: An angel that is with you throughout your life. Assisting you even before you think to ask.

Hologram: Energy creates, stores and retrieves meaning in the Universe by projecting or expanding at certain frequencies in a three-dimensional mode that creates a living pattern called a hologram.

Intuitive: Can be described as having a highly evolved sense of everything that lies beyond the five senses. Able to engage their well developed intuition to elevate their capacity for receiving images and other messages through dreams and through everyday occurrences.
Issues: beliefs or views that have led to fixed and often debilitating actions or inactions.

GLOSSARY

Joy of Creativity Workshops: Workshops to enable students to sculpt their own Angel Doll. Workshops where participants uncover unique gifts…and find the courage to pursue them and come to understand the ripple effect of healing within their immediate families, and beyond.

Knowing: An absolute surety, a total trust in what you recognize as truth. Knowing exists only in the total alignment of mind, body, and spirit…the holy trinity…

Lifetimes: All the lifetimes we have lived based on an understanding of reincarnation, but not confined to.

Personal Mindsets: of, or belonging to, a particular person; a set of attitudes or views formed by earlier events.

Realms: other dimensions, other energy frequencies, dimensions going beyond what is physically seen or understood on this earth plane.
Remembering: Within us we have the knowledge of all that is within the Hologram of Self. Of that which is known as Akashic records. *See in glossary under Akashic Records*
Reincarnation: The belief that after we die our soul returns, reborn again in another body, over multiple lifetimes.

Soul family: A family of souls that are familiar in vibration & intent. Shared many lifetimes, as in reincarnation.
Source: The great mystery…God…Creator.
Specific Time Frame: Specified place and happening. An event, an experience on a person's journey in this or other lifetimes.
Synchronise: to join with similar or parallel energies or beliefs coming together to occur or operate at the same time or rate.

*Unique vibration: your vibration, a vibration that is specific to an individual. Your personal fingerprint.
*Universally Inspired: Influenced by the whole of the universe, beyond earth, realms, without boundaries.
Universe: everything that exists. All that is, or ever has been.

Vibration: An energy connection/frequency – the energy emitted of anything i.e., person, angel, object. distinctive to an individual, like a fingerprint.

ABOUT THE AUTHORS

Sandra and Elsie

ELSIE POLIQUIN

Elsie Mary Bartzack-McGeough- Poliquin: An *intuitive* with a special affinity for angels, the life of plants, and the hearts of humanity. A consummate artist. A gleaner of knowledge and information which aided her success. Elsie is the proud mother of five beautiful children: Dean, Angela, Maureen, Frank and Ella Dawn. Grandmother of seven to Julie, Jonathan, Jenna Lea, Heidi, Joshua, Justin and Kristy. Great Grandmother to Nolan, Walker, Natalie, Levi, Gregory, Morgan, Finn, Dean and Isabella.

August 25, 1942, Elsie Mary was born in Kindersley, Alberta to a Canadian-born mother and an immigrated father. A tragic coal mining explosion that injured Elsie's father, forced Elsie's young mother, Annie, to move to Saskatchewan. It was to be the aunt and uncle in Elsie's new home that gave her a foundation. A true respect for the land, the open hearts of farming people and their Ukrainian/ Polish Culture. Elsie's interest in observing different religions is rooted in her attending the Roman Catholic Church during her formative years.

In Elsie's marriage, she pursued small-income ventures to assist in the support of her husband and family. A divorce, after her fifth child, led Elsie to create an independent source of income. The love of Arts & Craft determined the path she would take. Much to Elsie's surprise and delight she was successful at making salt-dough Clown Dolls! (Wholesaling from Greenwich Village, NY to Alaska).

In time Elsie became involved with the Healing Arts. The Energetic Healing work Elsie provided her clients was a new and uncharted path. With the evolution of her skills, Elsie began to sculpt doll-like figures and faces while contemplating a visual representation of peoples' Guardian Angels.

Elsie joined the angels in their realm on June 15, 2018. Not truly gone…and most certainly not forgotten…

SANDRA ANNE DAVIS

Sandra Anne Price-Davis was born in Fredericton, New Brunswick. At an early age her family moved to Toronto, Ontario, where she was raised and educated. Sandra's professional career has been long and diverse. Work for the Federal and Provincial government was distinguished by a continuous association over two decades with Centennial College. First as Director of Student Entrance Testing and Evaluation and ending as Director of the Wellness Centre.

Sandra was determined to integrate her skills and expand her knowledge. Further courses of study led Sandra to live & work throughout Canada & the United States. During the tenure of her Management Company in Florida, Sandra observed a noticeable shift in her perception of business and its expression in the world.

On her return to Canada, Sandra resolved to follow this newly found internal compass. Settling in Vancouver, British Columbia opened her to the world of Native Practitioners and traditional psychologists. Gifts of spiritual teachings and traditional Sweat lodges became her church…

Equipped with a revised knowledge of the world through the ways of the Medicine Wheel, Sandra followed her guidance to return to Toronto, Ontario where she founded and administered "The Womans' Lodge, a Pathway to Healing for All" in Toronto's beaches.

Through her business acumen, Sandra developed and honed the skills and diversity evidenced in all aspects of her life. A Reiki Master and Spiritual Counsellor with an international clientele, Sandra now resides with her husband Rick in their home in rural New Brunswick. Here she continues to offer her counselling services as she pursues her lifelong love of writing.

www.writingfortheloveofit.com

ACKNOWLEDGMENTS

Sincere gratitude and thanksgiving to those of you who assisted with this project…beginning and ending with the angels! My earth angels of the early days, Elsie, Linda Penn, and Inga were joined by the angelic realm, in a true collaboration of Joy! I wrote, Inga edited…we were excited! Fun and love and laughter permeated every minute we spent together.

One of our finest hours with Inga was the celebration of her 80th birthday. Together, with many of her wonderful friends, we all provided Inga with a gift from her bucket list. The opportunity to swim with dolphins in the wild off the coast of Florida. She had the time of her life!

After the death of our dear friend Inga and subsequent passing of our Elsie Mary, much of the original passion and enthusiasm waned for me. It seemed no matter how much work and effort I put into finishing the original manuscript, it wasn't working. I was determined not to let Elsie or Inga down…

Then it hit me! The realisation that our original book no longer existed. I now felt a new enthusiasm to create a different book. One that would honour Elsie and her unique angel sculptures. I was able to incorporate much of my early writings while directing the light where it belonged, on Elsie and her Angel Dolls.

I would be remiss not to acknowledge the assistance of my sister Jan and her insightfulness. Elsie's children, Maureen and Dean, for supplying much needed angel pictures and other family information. Bless all of you! May this book provide the honouring of your dear mother and my friend, Elsie Mary Poliquin.

Thank you, my dear Emma Pickering, for your editing and above all your unwavering patience with this entire project. And thank you to Greg Salisbury of Red Tuque Publishing, for your patience and book design expertise. Together, the three of us made up the sacred collaborative trifecta that would push this book towards the finish line.

Speaking of patience, kudos to my husband Rick! You fed me food and drink and other delightful nourishment throughout this entire labour of love! Honey, I will find a way to express my gratitude.

ENDNOTES

[i] ENERGY

The basic component of the Universe, energy, occurs in either unformed or materialised form. The things that we see around us, such as cars, houses, books, and trees, are examples of materialised energy. All energy that is not in materialised form makes up the balance of the energy in the Universe. Both states of energy are more similar in form than appears to the naked eye. Even those objects that seem most solid, such as steel beams and concrete walls, appear as molecules in motion when viewed under high-powered microscopes. All energy vibrates. The lower the vibration, the more density there is within the form. The higher the vibration, the more expansive the energy within the form.

What else do we know about energy? Since the Universe is energy, we are always interacting with it. Generally speaking, there are two ways to interact with energy. We can either align with the energy flowing around and through us, or we can resist the flow of that energy. We resist the flow of energy when we choose to interpret life in ways that lead us to struggle not only with the natural abundance all around us but with each other. Resisting the flow of energy lowers our vibration and causes us discomfort. On the other hand, when we choose to align with the free flow of energy, we feel at peace. In this state of free-flowing energy and peacefulness, we are open to the infinite Intelligence of the Universe, which is contained in all energy. Because we are all composed of energy, this Intelligence is always available to us. Accepting the fact that this Intelligence is always available to us encourages us to open ourselves to it. We feel and hear this Intelligence when our minds are quiet, and we are in a state of inner calmness. It is also in this state of inner calmness that we allow ourselves to feel our essence-the love that we truly are. Love is synonymous with energy. Our willingness to feel love, for ourselves and others, opens us not only to Infinite Intelligence but also to the unlimited abundance of the Universe. Let me suggest a scene to remind you of the Infinite supply of energy-love-that is always available to you to support the quality of life that you desire. See yourself in a sandbox at an ocean beach. Your sandbox is filled with sand, and there are miles of sandy beach in three directions. You give out pails of sand from your sandbox to passers-by. As your supply is depleted, you reach out and refill the box with the unlimited supply of sand that is all around you.

Our Universe is always ready to provide for us whenever we reach out to it. We need only understand the principles by which it operates, and then live by these principles. As we choose to live by Universal Principles, we experience the ease and grace of energy flowing freely around and through us, conversely, when we select guidelines that are at variance with Universal Principles, we experience the struggle and effort of resisting the natural flow of life. While the choice is always ours, it is helpful to know that our Infinite Intelligence is always there to encourage us to choose the natural order.

YOU CAN HAVE IT ALL
Arnold M. Patent (page 11 & 12)
Beyond Words Publishing Inc.
4443. NE Airport Road
Hillsboro, Oregon 97124-6074 ©1995

ii SAINT FRANCIS XAVIER

Born in the family castle of Xavier, near Pamplona in Basque area of Spanish Navarre on April 7, he was sent to the University of Paris, secured his licentiate in 1528, and met Ignatius Loyola! Francis became one of the seven who in 1534, at Montmartre founded the society of Jesus ORDER OF THE JESUITS! In 1536 Francis joined Ignatius in Venice and was ordained in 1537, went to Rome in 1538. In 1540 the pope formally recognized the Society and ordered Francis and FR. Simon Rodriguez, to the Far East as the first Jesuit missionaries. King John III kept FR. Simon in Lisbon, but Francis, after a year's voyage, six months of which were spent at Mozambique where he preached and gave aid to the sick, eventually arrived in Goa, India in 1542 with FR. Paul of Camerino, an Italian, and Francis Mansihas, a Portuguese. There he began preaching to the natives and attempted to reform his fellow Europeans, living among the natives and adopting their customs on his travels. During the next decade he converted tens of thousands to Christianity. He visited the Paravas at the tip of India, near Cape Comorin, Tuticorin (1542), Malacca (1545), the Moluccas near New Guinea Morotai near the Philippines (1546-47), and Japan (1549-51). In 1551, India and the East were set up as a separate province and Ignatius made Francis its first provincial. In 1552 he set out for China, landed on the island of Sancian within sight of his goal, but died before he reached the mainland. Working against great difficulties, language problems (contrary to legend, he had no proficiency in foreign tongues), inadequate funds, and lack of cooperation, often actual resistance from European Officials, he left the mark of his missionary zeal and energy on areas which clung to Christianity for centuries. He was canonised in 1622 and proclaimed patron of all foreign missions by Pope Pius X. F. D. Dec. 3.
©1997 CATHOLIC ONLINE. www.catholic.org.

ENDNOTES

iii CHAKRA:
Our etheric bodies contain major energy centres, located along an axis parallel to the spinal column of the physical body. These centres are called chakras, which means wheel or vortex......The chakras absorb higher energy from the Universe and step it down to a usable level for us on the physical plane. Our endocrine system assists the chakras in converting these higher vibrations into accessible energy. The chakras also work individually and collectively to keep the physical, emotional, and spiritual selves functioning optimally, in harmony with one another and the Universe.
Crystal Deva Cards
Cindy Watlington (page 43 & 44)
Inner Quest publishing
Box 17234
Boulder, Colorado 80308

iv MI'KMAQ
Also spelled MI'KMAQ, the largest of the Native American (First Nations) people traditionally occupying what are now Canada's eastern Maritime Provinces (Nova Scotia, New Brunswick, and Prince Edward Island) and parts of the present US states of Maine and Massachusetts.….The name Mi'kmaq derives from the term nikmaq, meaning "my kin-friends" and also the greeting "my brothers!" in the 1600s. The singular form of the word is Mi'kmaw. The word "Mi kmaq" is never used as an adjective.
www.britannica.com

www.ingramcontent.com/pod-product-compliance
Lightning Source LLC
Chambersburg PA
CBHW050746110526
44590CB00003B/92